DESTINATION LAPLAND

By the same author

Five Hundred Mile Walkies

Destination Lapland
A Journey to the Far North

MARK WALLINGTON

HUTCHINSON
London Melbourne Auckland Johannesburg

Copyright © Mark Wallington 1987

All rights reserved

This edition first published in 1987 by Hutchinson Ltd, an imprint of Century
Hutchinson Ltd, Brookmount House, 62–65 Chandos Place, London WC2N 4NW

Century Hutchinson Australia Pty Ltd
PO Box 496, 16–22 Church Street, Hawthorn, Victoria 3122, Australia

Century Hutchinson New Zealand Limited
PO Box 40–086, Glenfield, Auckland 10, New Zealand

Century Hutchinson South Africa (Pty) Ltd
PO Box 337, Bergvlei, 2012 South Africa

British Library Cataloguing in Publication Data
Wallington, Mark
Destination Lapland: a journey to the far north.
1. England — Description and travel — 1971-
I. Title
914.2′04858   DA632

ISBN 0 09 170700 5

Set in Bembo by Avocet Marketing Services, Bicester, Oxon
Printed and bound in Great Britain by Anchor Brendan Ltd, Tiptree, Essex

To Dick Fiddy,
who has only ever bored me once
– last summer it was, in a Turkish restaurant in
Maida Vale

Acknowledgements

Many thanks to Steve Smith, Jill Hobart, Ned and Edna Hill, Jim Beck and Stephanie Shields, and especially to Susan Aspinall.

Contents

1. First squashed hedgehog
2. First squashed stoat
3. First squashed rabbit
4. First squashed Ford Sierra
5. Back axle snapped
6. Excellent salad sandwich
7. Did very well in Fell race
8. First squashed toad
9. Marks & Spencer
10. Chain broke first time
11. Chain broke second time
12. Chain broke third time
13. Fortieth squashed hedgehog
14. Chain broke fourth time
15. Bought new chain
16. First squashed rat
17. David Gower scores a century
18. Hurricane and first puncture
19. First squashed jelly fish
20. Collision with Bamburgh Castle
21. Thirty seventh fried egg since St Albans

18 BERWICK-UPON-TWEED
17 JEDBURGH •
19 HOLY ISLAND
20 BAMBURGH
16 BELLINGHAM •
ALNMOUTH
BRAMPTON •
21. NEWCASTLE
• 15 CARLISLE
• 14 SILLOTH
• 13 WIGTON
• 12 APPLEBY
• 11 SEDBERGH
• 10 HAWES
• MALHAM
• SKIPTON
9 BLACKPOOL •
BRADFORD •
MANCHESTER •
• 8 BATLEY
• HOLMFIRTH
• BRADWELL
7 BRASSINGTON
6 ASHBOURNE
• 5 ROCESTER
• IRONBRIDGE
• 4 BISHOP'S CASTLE
LUDLOW •
3 TENBURY WELLS
STRATFORD ON AVON
2 KINETON •
• 1 MILTON KEYNES
ST ALBANS •

1. Hertfordshire: Buying a Bicycle

Before setting off for Lapland, always have a haircut – not an essential part of the preparation for such a trip, but a useful one nevertheless. A haircut has inspirational qualities. It changes the shape of the face. It refreshes; creates a new identity. You slump into the swivel chair feeling unmotivated, your head in a knot, emerging half an hour later with your apprehensions scattered on the lino beneath you in little hairy heaps. There's a sense of purpose sitting on your head and journeys to places like Lapland seem suddenly possible.

Of course, this all rather depends on where you get your hair cut.

I used to be a regular at Mario and Mo's, an Italian hairdressers behind the station in St. Albans. A sign outside said, 'Gents Salon', but Mario and Mo's was the coiffured equivalent of a transport cafe; it smelt of Vosene and ragout Bolognese. On the wall was a picture of Tony Curtis. Brylcreem leaked like salad dressing from bottles on the counter. A faded advert for Silvikrin hair tonic stood in the window next to the 'Early Closing On Wednesdays' sign, and on the mirror were autographed photos of the AC Milan team that beat Leeds United 1-0 in the 1973 European Cup Winners Cup Final (Chiarugi, 35 min.).

Mario and Mo were brothers they said, although Mario was tall and bald and Mo was short and hairy. It was always Mo who saw to me. He wore a white T-shirt with tufts of black hair crawling out through the neck, and as he worked he talked about Calabria, about his mountain childhood, about his dream of a villa on the Gulf of Taranto, and about why Italians have such bad dandruff problems. A visit to Mario and Mo's was more than just a haircut. It was a journey around the toe of Italy with two genuine and interesting people. Unfortunately, they were lousy at cutting hair, really lousy.

So I shopped around, went upmarket. My next ten haircuts were in places with names like Shapes, Scalps, Snippers, Snappers and Uppercuts; all salons in pedestrian precincts with yucca plants in the window, and staffed by women with name tags pinned to their chests. My hair looked better but my imagination suffered and so when I needed somewhere to get my head in shape for a trip beyond the Arctic Circle it was no surprise to find myself instinctively heading back over the railway bridge to Mario and Mo's.

Sadly, during my absence someone had turned it into a Tandoori take-away and so I had to settle for a garish little salon called His and Hers Trendicuts on the London Road. I leaned my luggage-laden bicycle against the window and presented myself to a girl wearing a Lorraine badge.

'I'm going to Lapland and I'd like a cut and blow dry, please.'

'Yes sir,' said Lorraine, 'Sharon will look after you.'

Sharon led me over to a basin in the corner. 'Did you watch the royal wedding?' she said.

'No-one puts on a show of pageantry like the British.' I replied.

'I think foreigners are just a little bit jealous of our royal family. What shampoo would you prefer: verbena and lemon balm or wheatgerm and rowanberry?'

'You decide.'

'Just put your head back then.' And as Sharon pulled me

down by the hair and dunked me in the basin, I could see right down her tunic, and the view summed up perfectly why Mario and Mo's is now a Tandoori take-away.

The year has always had a definite shape for me. I've often asked people if it has for them too but their answers are normally vague, a circle perhaps or just a straight line. For me though, it's always had a parabolic appearance; it's coloured as well. It begins in January, grey and faded, sloping gently into the spring where the colours suddenly become vivid and contrasted. The summer is a hazy yellow trough and then in September it begins to climb again, steeply and darkly towards the starry peak of Christmas.

When rewound, my memory always settles in one of those summer troughs. The seemingly endless school holidays, a balmy eight weeks of Aertex shirts and green knees. And even now, when the schools break up and the town centres become full of kids roaming round the precincts pulling the nasturtiums out of the ornamental tubs, I grow restless. I wake up early and have pangs of anticipation. It's the summer holidays and I shouldn't be sitting at a desk staring at a wall.

But this summer was going to be all work. I had a TV series to write. I'd resigned myself to spending July, August and September locked in a room with a scriptwriting partner, trying desperately not to turn on the Test Match. Then the TV series was thrown out. One phone call and I had the whole summer. I had no ties and no commitments; the next entry in my diary was a Guy Fawkes party. The sudden freedom was overwhelming and a journey was my first thought. A summer's journey. A slow summer's journey. I opened the window and surveyed the warm blue July sky. A bus to Luton motored past. A bus journey would be a good idea. A bicycle followed the bus. A bicycle journey would be even better. A lorry from Hunts Haulage Ltd followed the bicycle, caught it in its slipstream and sent the cyclist into the back of a Ford Sierra with an 'I have seen the Lions of Longleat' sticker in the window. Maybe a lorry journey would be the best of all.

But where to? A journey had to have a destination, surely. When you announce your imminent departure on a trip, the obvious response is 'where to?', and you tend to lose credibility if you're stumped for an answer. But I was tired of destinations; the idea of them no longer excited me the way it once had. I've come to realise that when I travel I'm not that bothered about where I'm going. The journey itself is the thing. If I have a destination, by the time I get there I've built up such a detailed picture of the place I know exactly how it ought to be. And then of course I'm always disappointed. I can't help it. The appetite I have for travel is never satisfied by arrival. I prefer climbing on a bus rather than climbing off. I feel more excited in departure lounges than in Arrivals. This time, I decided, what I wanted more than a destination was a direction.

That summer, as every summer, everyone seemed to be heading south. I think the Greeks had discovered a new island, or perhaps they'd built one. In England the perennial traffic jams crawled towards the south coast and the channel ferries. Whenever I see a queue of cars I'm always reminded of an advertisement for a brand of petrol that used to run years ago. It featured a raised motorway running through a city. In one direction, the one into the city centre, the three lanes are solid with traffic; in the other they're empty but for one car with a tankful of the appropriate fuel which motors unhindered out of the metropolis. I always imagined the queue to be facing south, the lone car heading north. North was wild, open country. It made me think of moorland and industry, Vikings and icebergs. It sounded like my sort of place.

So I took out an atlas and followed roads up through

England to Newcastle, on to Edinburgh, no, not Edinburgh, every one man band went to Edinburgh in the summer, I'd continue north into Scandinavia, take a boat to Bergen then follow the west coast of Norway up over the Arctic Circle and on finally to where I ran out of road near the town of Hammerfest on the North Cape in the area known as Lapland. Lapland? If I had to have a destination that was the sort I could handle. I knew nothing about the place other than it was roughly fifteen hundred miles away and Father Christmas lived there. It wasn't a country or a town, it was a zone. Not so much a destination as a target area. I went to the library and borrowed the only book on Lapland they had. On the front cover was a picture of a reindeer and a man in a ludicrous hat. I liked the look of the place already. 'The land of the Lapps is a magical world,' said the first sentence and I was sold.

I made hurried plans. I would go by bicycle, I decided. It was the sort of pace I wanted, and traffic I could avoid by sticking to B roads. I'd give myself two months: forty miles a day, surely I could manage that? It was four years since my last journey of any exertion and I'd hardly lifted a leg since, but I would use England to prepare myself. Instead of cycling to Newcastle straight up the flat east side of the country, I'd get myself fit for the fjords by heading out over the Pennines and the Northern counties. I wanted to keep reminding myself, this was a trip north not just a head-down sprint for the Arctic. Anyway, I'd plan it all as I went along. I was excited by the sudden prospect of the whole summer to myself and I didn't want to linger. All I had to do was to get my bicycle out of the ... out of the ... it was then I realised I didn't have a bicycle.

'Summer Second Hand Bike Bonanza', said the sign outside the local scout hut. 'Saturday. One o'Clock'.

And I was there on the dot only to find everyone else had

got there at twelve and the only bikes left were the lame and infirm. A thirteen-year-old and his dad were conducting the sale. They were a cycling family. They had shaved legs and appeared to be very tall, although in fact what they were was long.

'I'd like a touring bicycle please,' I said.

'Are you married?' said the dad.

'What!'

'Are you married?'

'No.'

'Engaged, perhaps?'

'No!'

'Courting, maybe?'

'I only want a touring bicycle.'

'You wouldn't be interested in a tandem then? Ninety-five quid to you.'

'Oh, I see.' Behind him, leaning sadly against the wall, was an ancient tandem. It looked like a lump of scaffolding on wheels.

'Eddie and Mrs Mercx used to have one like this,' said the son.

'Sorry. I'm single.' I said.

'I'm not surprised,' said the dad.

'What do you mean?'

'Well you haven't got a tandem, have you? I mean, if you met a woman, how would you take her out?'

'I've got a Triumph.'

'Yeah, well, Triumphs are all very well but if you really want to impress a woman ... tell you what, eighty quid and it's yours.'

'I don't want a tandem. I'm travelling alone.'

'You can pick up hitch-hikers on a tandem. Seventy quid and that's my last offer.'

'What's that bike over there?' I asked. A green, muscular

machine had caught my eye. If I collided with a car on something like that the car would have come off worse.

'Thirty quid,' said the dad.

'Claud Butler used to have one just like this,' said the son.

I demurred. On closer inspection I doubted it would get me home, let alone to Lapland. I asked what the strange spring loaded grip on the front fork was for.

'It's a tennis racket holder,' said the dad.

'I don't play tennis.'

'Doesn't matter, it's broken,' said the son.

I rode the sad machine down the gravel path. It was a bike with no pretensions, no accessories and, as I discovered when I tried to stop at the main road, no brakes. I wheeled it back to the hut.

'Listen, I want something that's going to get me as far as the Arctic Circle. I've got fifty quid.'

'Well why didn't you say?' said the dad. 'Got just the bike for you.'

'I've told you I don't want a tandem.'

'No, no. I'm talking about the Arctic Circle Tourer. Go and get the Arctic Circle Tourer, son.'

'Which one's that?' said the boy.

'The red one.'

'You can't sell him that.'

'Why not?'

'It's mine. You gave it me for Christmas.'

Smack!

The boy disappeared into a back room. 'Yes, I think you'll like the Arctic Circle Tourer,' said the dad. 'Costs fifty quid by the way, which is a bit of a coincidence, isn't it. What with you having fifty quid to spend. No tennis racket holder though.'

The Arctic Circle Tourer turned out to be a rather more sleek model: ten gears, a new saddle and a reasonable frame decorated with a selection of free-with-Shredded-Wheat spacecraft transfers. I cycled it down the gravel path and it got me back to the hut again without any major mechanical malfunction. I was impressed.

'£50. It's a snip for an Arctic Circle Tourer,' said the dad. 'It's even got a bell.'

I could patch it up, I thought; give it a service. I flicked the bell. There was the sound of rust scrapping rust from inside.

'All right, £49.50,' said the dad. 'Tell you what, give us ninety quid and I'll throw in the tandem.'

'No thanks.'

'You could start a mini-cab service with a tandem.'

No thanks.'

I hate giving machines names, but the next day as I sat looking at the bike in bits all around me I found myself continually calling my Arctic Circle Tourer, You Bastard. I couldn't understand it. It had come apart so easily.

And I really didn't want to be doing with all this. I just wanted to get going. I threw it back together. I'd service it properly, bit by bit, en route. The same principle went for any specialist equipment I might need: I'd buy it as and when I needed it. I wanted to carry as little as possible. Anything vaguely superfluous was discarded. Maps, for instance. I've never liked the idea of travelling with maps; they take the spontaneity out of a journey. I like travelling without clues. If my plan was to head north all I needed as a navigational aid was a compass. Maps could go. I filled their space with a jar of Marmite.

The only luxury items I took were a trendy sapphire blue pullover with a black fleck from Al's Garage Boutique – which may not sound like recommended Arctic Circle attire, but I was sick of going on these trips dressed like a slob in boots and baggy jumpers and checked shirts from Milletts. The Lapps were a colourful lot by the look of them and I wanted to fit in – and a Norwegian phrase book which I

planned to study on the way up through England, becoming
fluent enough to ask where the opera house is when I finally
reached the North Cape. I found one in the local library.
While I was there I renewed my Lapland guide book.

'I'd like to take these books out for eight weeks, please.'

'Impossible,' said the librarian, the big one, the big ugly,
mean one, 'you'll have to renew them after four.'

'I'm going to Lapland.'

'You'll have to come back then, won't you.'

'It's fifteen hundred miles away.'

'Can't help that, someone else might want them.'

'This one's not been taken out since March 1977.'

'I was thinking of going to Lapland myself this summer as
it happens.'

'What if I don't bring them back for eight weeks?'

'We give your name and address to Mrs Broadbent in
reference.'

'Oh yeah? And she comes and finds me I suppose?'

'No, she goes and burns your house down. Back here
August the fifteenth, or else!' He stamped the books. The
desk shuddered. They're a tough lot down my library.

What would Magellan have done if his library had
ordered him to return his true adventure books after four
weeks? What would Hillary have said, if he'd been
threatened with fines of sixpence a day rising to twenty-five
pence after a fortnight, for letting his science fiction go
overdue? Doubtless they'd have done what I did: asked a
friend to renew by telephone after four weeks, the same
friend I asked to look after my house plants, the same friend
who lent me a soap dish, the same friend I sat next to in The
Blue Boar on the afternoon of July 23.

'Did you watch the royal wedding?' asked Linda.

Prince Andrew and Sarah Ferguson had been married that
morning. Television coverage had begun at 6.15 a.m. with
interviews of countless old ladies from Sevenoaks who'd

camped outside the palace for two nights and eaten nothing but Batchelors Cupasoup. The Stockwell Strangler and the Commonwealth Games boycott had been forgotten for the day as high streets were decked out in red white and blue, and everyone sat in front of televisions and in pubs saying things like: 'no-one puts on a spectacle of pageantry like the British,' and 'you know, I think foreigners are just a bit jealous of our royal family.'

'No-one puts on a spectacle of pageantry like the British,' I said.

'You know, I think foreigners are just a bit jealous of our royal family,' said Linda.

The school holidays had just begun. The pub was full of teachers. They all looked smug with the whole summer in front of them. Before, it used to annoy me but now I felt smug as well. Two friends, one who looks like Charlie Drake, the other like Bamber Gascoigne, were standing at the bar talking about word processors:

'You see, Control-C normally stops the current program and returns you to Direct Mode, whereas Control-S just suspends the current program until another key is pressed,' said Charlie Drake.

'Oh,' said Bamber Gascoigne.

'Now, after an option run command neither key has any effect, furthermore the program will run faster, see?' said Charlie Drake.

'Right,' said Bamber Gascoigne.

'So, that means usually basic will check the keyboard getting a system dependent over head,' said Charlie Drake.

'Bye then,' I said.

'What?' said Bamber Gascoigne.

'I'm going to Lapland.'

'Are you?' said Charlie Drake. 'Bye then. Give my regards to the Arctic Circle ... now, you see basic's random

number generator produces a pseudo random sequence ...
Lapland?'

'Yes.'

'It's a good place to get a reindeer hatstand, that is,' said
Charlie Drake.

I was given all sorts of useful advice like that:

'Discos are expensive in Norway.'

'Thanks, I'll remember that.'

'It's halfday closing in Oslo on Thursday.'

'Thanks, I'll remember that.'

'I've got a friend in Bergen. His name's Stig.'

'Thanks, I'll remember that.'

'That's a horrible pullover.'

'Thanks, I'll remember that.'

My phrase book came out. It was suddenly very funny to
speak in Scandinavian accents. Someone asked if they
wanted to contact me should they write a letter and send it
up the chimney. As the bell went for last orders Linda took
me aside, kissed me gently and said: 'Come back safely,
won't you.'

My mind worked fast.

'I don't have to go just now, you know. I could hang
around for a couple of days. I'm in no hurry.'

'No, you must go.'

'Must I?'

'Yes. But promise me one thing ... '

'Anything ... '

'If you do make it. If you do manage to cycle your little
bike as far as Lapland. And if you do manage to come all the
way back and get the return boat ... '

'Yes ... '

'You will get me a bottle of duty free perfume, won't you?
Diorissimo. Here, I'll write it down. 90 ml bottle will do.'

At three thirty I climbed onto my bike, and, with a
valediction: *Jeg vil gjerne at mottakeren betaler*,' which I thought

meant: 'Goodbye and good health,' but in fact meant: 'I'd like to reverse the charges,' I pedalled off in the general direction of the Arctic.

My head was pulled out of the water. I rubbed the soap out of my eyes. Sharon had gone. In her place I could see a small dark man in a bib. His badge said, George.

'Watch the royal wedding?' he said.

'No-one puts on a spectacle of pageantry like the British,' I replied.

'You know, I think foreigners are just a little bit jealous of our royal family.' His accent was clipped. I asked him where he was from.

'Gibraltar,' he said, 'do you want conditioner? It's self-adjusting.'

'You decide.' He slapped some on and I thought: fantastic! I've only been on the road ten minutes and I'm already having a Gibraltarian rub self-adjusting conditioner into my head. This is what international travel is all about.

I was led over to a chair next to Mrs Bunnage. In the mirror, I could see her perusing a magazine with a picture of Souxie and the Banshees on the cover. A girl labelled Rosemary was standing over her. Mrs Bunnage pointed to the picture of Souxie and said: 'I'd like it like this only purpler.'

A girl called Carol was suddenly standing at my shoulder, scissors poised: 'How do you want it, then?'

'You decide.'

The scissors went to work. I watched her in the mirror. She was cutting my hair and looking out of the window at the traffic. I thought: she must be a really good hairdresser to do that.

'Been on your holidays yet?' she said, diving into the standard hairdresser's script at the first page to fall open.

'Just off. Off to Lapland. That's my bike outside. Off to the

North Cape. The land of the Lapps is a magical place, you know.'

'Wanna cup of coffee?'

'You decide.'

She walked off and came back with a cup of coffee. Hairs floated on the surface. I wouldn't have minded but they weren't mine.

'Lapland? That's north isn't it?'

'Northish.'

'Birmingham way?'

'Further.'

'Leeds?'

'Further.'

'Up round the Arctic Circle then?'

'That's right.'

'I cut an Eskimo's hair once. At least he said he was an Eskimo. He had a funny nose I know that. Talk about unmanageable. His hair I mean. Like glass it was. How much off the back?'

'You decide.' Next to me Mrs Bunnage was growing purpler and purpler.

'What plug sizes to they have in Lapland?' asked Carol.

Plug sizes weren't something I'd thought about. The previous evening I'd read my book, *The Lapps*, until the early hours and discovered that Lapland comprised a crescent-shaped area stretching from the rugged coast of Norway across the top of Sweden, Finland and the Soviet Union as far east as the Kola Peninsula on the White Sea. I'd also discovered the Lapps wear string vests all the year round, that their traditional music is vocal rather than instrumental, and that a typical freight *pulka* (boat sledge) is about two metres long with a maximum width of twenty inches. As for Lapp plug sizes, though, I had to admit I was totally in the dark. This concerned Carol greatly:

'You can't be too careful,' she said. 'I went to Skiathos last year. Voltage in the hotel was 220 AC with a 60 watt cycle. Two-pin plugs on top of that. And there's me with my 240 volt Morphy Richards. I had to fork out five thousand drachmas on a Braun Independent. Runs on Butane. How much off the front?'

'You decide.'

Actually I hoped plug sizes in Lapland were different. Different from any plug sizes I'd ever come across before. Weren't those little idiosyncrasies of a country once the attraction of travel? Soon plug sizes would be the only way to tell one place fron another: 'Ah! 250 volts with a two-pin. This must be Chile!'

In the mirror I could see Mrs Bunnage disappear under a dome. Electrical leads sprung out from her head in Franken-stein fashion. Rosemary flicked the switch and Mrs Bunnage started to buzz and hum. Becoming purple isn't as straightforward as it looks.

Carol stood back from my head and held the mirror up behind me. 'Is that all right?' she asked.

It's always a shock when you see the back of your own head. The hair on one side was longer than the other. The back was jagged. Some bits stood out at right angles. The top was cut to make it look as though I was wearing a crash helmet. Behind the ear nearest to Mrs Bunnage I had a purple patch.

'That's fine,' I said.

There's always something inauspicious about the start of a long and memorable journey. Imagine Magellan having to cancel the milk and newspapers the day he left to circumnav-igate the globe. Or Hillary standing at the bus stop outside his house on the first leg of his journey to base camp in '53. Likewise, my trip to Lapland began with a right turn past Harris Furnishings, on past Freeman Grieve the chemist, over the traffic lights and onto the A6 towards Luton.

A breezy, sunny afternoon, cars with their tops down, the green verges spilling onto the pavement. An aeroplane bound for Corfu left a white tail of fuel in the sky and I stopped at a Pick Your Own fruit farm and filled a bag of strawberries for almost nothing. I was rolling along, riding high on the thrill of departure, and I barely heard the metallic clank as something fell off my rear and bounced under a Matthews Pressed Turkey lorry. Immediately, my back wheel began to shudder, my chain slipped, my ten speed turned into a two speed and when I pulled my brakes there was little response. Teething problems that's all, I told myself, and continued into Bedfordshire. But when my knees started to make the same grinding noise as my crank and then just outside Luton a pedestrian overtook me, I realised repairs were necessary and I limped to a friend's house in the village of Caddington.

It was 5 p.m. Ralph works nights and had just got up. He was sitting at the breakfast table reading the paper. The middle pages had a picture of Andrew and Fergie lookalikes in bed together on their wedding night.

'I've brought you some strawberries,' I said, and dumped a soggy red plastic bag on the table.

Ralph looked at me through baggy eyes. He was really pleased to see me.

'That's a ridiculous pullover,' he said.

'You don't mind if I stay the night, do you?'

'Not half as ridiculous as your haircut, mind.'

'You don't mind if I fix my bike in your living room, do you?'

He didn't say anything. He was still half asleep. I went to watch the royal wedding highlights on television. Half an hour later I heard him shout something. A car door slammed, an engine revved and I was left alone for the evening with the bicycle maintenance book I'd bought in Harpenden and the Sainsbury's cheese and bacon flan I'd found in the fridge.

'A bicycle is a precision piece of engineering, not unlike the human body', the book's introduction said, in which case I had one very ill bike.

'Chapter One: Buying a Bicycle: beware of secondhand sales; never buy a bike off a man with shaved legs.' I flicked through the repair section. Every page stressed how simple it all was and then launched into instructions of the 'slot crank bolt B into pedal shaft F and introduce chainring G to large sprocket K,' variety. I decided I'd start with the derailleur:

'Undo cable bolt F ... '

I undid cable bolt F.

' ... Slip out mounting lock G ... '

I slipped out mounting lock G.

' ... Remove locknut L ... '

I removed locknut L, to the sound of spring S, axle nut N and adaptor screw O, flying across the room.

' ... having first ensured pivot bolts P and R are secure.'

I drew up a schedule. I'd work my way through the book as I travelled. By the time I reached Newcastle I wanted to know this machine inside out. But I'd start tomorrow. Tonight I wanted to dedicate to Norwegian. I opened my phrase book at the 'At the Theatre' section and practised in front of the mirror:

'Jeg vil gierne ha en losje til 4.'

('I'd like a box for 4.')

I looked at my hair. Lapland was the only sensible place to go with a cut like that.

'Kan De anbefale en western?'

('Can you recommend a western?')

A piece of paper floated from the back of the book. On it were written five names, familiar names. I suddenly remembered. Before I left I'd gone round the pub collecting sponsorship money. According to this account I'd raised the princely sum of £2.50. For the life of me though, I couldn't remember for which charity.

But I felt a responsibility to reach Lapland now. I learnt the Norwegian for, 'Can I have a ticket for the matinee on Tuesday,' is *'Kan jeg fa wn billett til matineen tirsdag'*, and then went to sleep on the couch, feeling the trip had a purpose at last. Ralph woke me when he came in at five a.m. He bounced into the room and threw back the curtains: 'It's a beautiful morning; sun's just up; birds and things are singing; just the day to begin a cycling holiday.'

'Get lost.'

Complete role reversal from the previous evening. I didn't want to move. He was hyperactive, and went upstairs with a couple of cans of beer to play his new bass guitar. Such is the upside-down world of the night worker.

I looked out of the window. It was indeed a lovely morning. And Ralph was right, the sun was just up and birds and things were singing. And there was an enormous amount of truth in the suggestion that this was the perfect day to begin a cycling holiday, even one to Lapland.

I winced at the prospect and curled up back on the couch.

2. Heart of England: Transmission

Following signs to Milton Keynes and filling my head with Lapland: the Lapps are traditionally nomads dependent on their reindeer herds; Lapland is the last great wilderness in Europe; the Lapp's name for themselves is Sameh; the Kola Lapps in Russia have been collectivised; the disease reindeer are most prone to is hoof-rot; in winter the sun disappears for seven weeks; in summer, at latitude 72 degrees N. it doesn't set for eighty-eight days; in winter the Lapps stay home and go to bed early; in summer they stay up late and play games; Blind Man's Buff is popular, cricket isn't.

It was entirely the opposite case at Lords that morning on the opening day of the First Test Match against New Zealand. I was cycling steadily through Bedfordshire villages towards Leighton Buzzard, my radio for company. 'The Stockwell Strangler strikes again' was the bad news. Brian Johnson introducing Test Match Special was the good.

The contest for the Best Kept Bedfordshire Village award of 1986 was well under way. 'The judges aren't necessarily looking for the prettiest village so much as the tidiest and best kept', the rules stated, and the result was that the houses didn't look lived in. Eaton Bray and Stanbridge seemed to be the fiercest competitors. All the villagers were mowing lawns and clipping hedges. Their gardens looked as though they were Hoovered each morning. You could imagine a provisional wing from each village planning nocturnal raids on the other; their aim to distribute litter, pull up geraniums and spray graffiti: 'Okay chaps, aerosols at the ready. And don't forget, Mr Forsythe, there are two Ls in Bollocks.'

Although it was operating at greatly reduced capacity, I'd botched my Arctic Circle Tourer sufficiently to ensure that it was at least mobile that morning. I was moving rather awkwardly but I'd begun to relearn how pleasant a pace to travel at cycling is. Fast enough to reach Buckinghamshire by lunchtime; slow enough to look at notice boards in villages, to watch the gliders soaring in ever decreasing circles over Dunstable Downs, to ponder on how on earth somewhere gets to be called Leighton Buzzard, and to become gradually more and more concerned as to whether or not I'd switched my oven off before I left home.

To discover the derivations of Leighton Buzzard I was quite prepared to sit down in the local history section of the reference library but instead I asked the assistant in Milletts. His response was:

'What?'

Followed by:

'Sorry mate. This is Milletts.'

'In that case,' I said, 'have you got a light-weight-one-man tent suitable for the Arctic Circle?' to which he also replied:

'What?'

Followed by:

'Sorry mate. This is Milletts.'

However, the man in the cycling shop where I stopped to buy a new locknut A and pivot bolt P for my derailleur was better informed. He put down his copy of *Bicycle Weekly* with the headline 'Cycling and Aids. Amazing new theory!' and told me that the parish of Leighton Buzzard was transferred from the diocese of Dorchester in Oxfordshire to Lincoln in 1189. But on discovering they had another Leighton on their books, the clerics of Lincoln attached the name of the parson of the time – Theobald de Busat – to Leighton, and the town

became known as Leighton Busat, which later became
Leighton Busard, which in turn became Leighton Buzzard.

'Anything else you want to know?' he said.

'Yes, how do you fix derailleurs?'

'I've got a golden rule for fixing derailleurs,' he said. '1/
Take them apart. 2/ put them back together. 3/ throw away
the bits.'

I'd swallowed my first insect of the trip coming down
Dunstable Downs. I was looking up at a hang-glider at the
time, – transfixed not so much by the pilot's aerobatical
expertise but by his ability to eat what appeared to be a
sandwich as he flew – when into my awestruck, open-
mouthed expression swooped something black and creepy
which buzzed like a bi-plane down past my epiglottis into the
graveyard of my stomach. Now I was cycling along the
Grand Union Canal towpath, and along these watery
breeding grounds, the insect population was ever larger and
more varied. Just past Leighton Linsdale I felt a thin hairy
object crawl down my throat, and then as the canal becomes
the River Ouzel, I swallowed my first blow-fly. All good
protein, I told myself, and kept on pedalling, but by the time
I stopped for lunch by the lock keeper's cottage at Leighton
Lock I'd lost my appetite.

I sat on the grass studying my derailleur, pork pie in one
hand, screw driver in the other: 'loosen locknut B; use a
metric Allen wrench to turn pivot A clockwise for more
tension; secure chain roller cage and unscrew stop bolt SB'.
This stuff was more confusing than Norwegian grammar.

A kettle sang in the lock-keeper's cottage; a narrow boat
chugged past with a dog at the controls; a plane bound for
Mykonos disappeared into cloud; England, having won the
toss, were cruising along at 96 for 1. Surely I switched my
oven off before I came out? Yes of course I did. I'd baked a
potato for lunch and I can remember removing it from the

oven and then taking a plate out of the cupboard, the polyunsaturated spread from the fridge and a knife from the drawer, and then I turned round and turned off the oven. No I didn't. When I took the spread out of the fridge, it was the fridge I turned off, to defrost. Then I went into the other room, sat down, ate the potato then ... ah yes ... of course, I came back into the kitchen, put the plate in the sink and switched off ... no, hang on, before I did that the phone rang. I remember I answered it and the caller said, 'Is that Timothy Whites?', and I said, 'No, wrong number,' and then ...

'Hadlee bowls a fuller length delivery, and Athey drives full bloodedly and he gets an edge and he's caught! Caught neatly in the gully by Jeff Crowe falling to his right, and England are 102 for 2.'

I screwed my derailleur back together. My two speed had now increased to a four speed. Only six more gears to find. I was getting there. It was then I noticed the bolt lying on the grass. What had the man in the shop said? 'Take it apart, put it back together and throw away the bits.' That was ridiculous. I pocketed the bolt, then threw the rest of my pork pie to the fish who threw it back, and pedalled off.

And if you're heading north, there are few better routes to follow than the Grand Union Canal. For two hundred years, until the 1950s, this link between the industrial north and London was a procession of barges and their butties; a constantly moving chain of coal and timber, powered in the early years by horses and later by steam, and crewed by a fraternity of bargees with a gypsy lifestyle.

Rail and road inevitably brought about the decline of the canals for commercial transport, only pleasure craft use them now; and yet I knew that no matter where I was as I journeyed north as far as Yorkshire, I would never be far away from one of these peaceful and echoful cuts. There could be motorways and railways running all around me but somewhere meandering through the countryside there'd be this still water life, and the low and rhythmic diesel beat of a method of transport spectacularly slow and outmoded but irresistible.

Not far from Leighton Locks I met a man standing proudly in the cockpit of a narrowboat called The Longevity. He and his wife had recently retired, he said, and they'd sold up their house and business and bought this forty-foot boat, surely a hot favourite for the Best Kept Narrowboat of the Year Award. It had a telephone, a microwave, water colours on the wall and had been fitted out by an interior designer. The way the owner spoke, even the bilge pump sounded elegant. The only thing it didn't appear to have was a garden.

'Want to see the garden?' he asked, and led me round the deck to some boxes of geraniums and some tomato plants sitting in a Gro-more bag.

'All I do now,' he said, 'is potter up and down these canals the year round. The wife navigates, I'm chief engineer. We used to live near Brands Hatch, see. Well, it was all this brmm, brmm, brmm every Bank Holiday. We couldn't hear ourselves think, so we bought Longevity here.'

'Doesn't it get cold in the winter?'

'I'll tell you what, last Christmas Day I had my Christmas dinner on the Liverpool-Leeds, with the snow falling outside, the oven full on and me sat in here with the window open . . . freezing it was.'

I asked him if he missed the South of England. Most of the interesting canals were in the North.

'Whenever we bring the boat back to London it costs us a fortune. It's the mooring, you see. Also the kids spit at you from the bridges and throw things, lumps of concrete for instance.'

He was a placid man. He couldn't be having lumps of concrete thrown at him. He'd never been happier than now, he said. He sat outside when he felt like it; he read when he felt like it. He loved his wife and he took all the time he wanted to do anything he liked.

I enjoyed cycling along the towpath. Travelling on or next to water involves seeing the land from a different perspective, and although canals cut into the countryside they manage to landscape themselves. It was with this peaceful riparian image that the new city of Milton Keynes had chosen to advertise itself. I'd seen the television commercial the previous evening. A man is filmed leaving his house at sunrise, fishing tackle slung over his shoulder. He cycles over bridges and alongside water meadows. The sound track is bird song. You get a brief view of a factory or two in the distance and then you're lost in the netherlands of the canal and the slogan appears: 'Wouldn't it be nice if all cities were like Milton Keynes?'

Actually it wouldn't, but approaching the city along the towpath this scripted image is just the one you get. Past Fenny Stratford, as ring roads and railways roar overhead, the canal is a shiny black worm sneaking up on the city. You're cycling innocently along, whistling, saying hello to the fishermen, listening to the Test Match, and then you see an exit from the towpath and you think: I wonder where that leads to?, and you pedal up it and at the top you must feel what a submarine captain feels when he surfaces in the middle of the enemy fleet. For there, suddenly all around you, as far as the eye can see, is Milton Keynes.

'*Milton Keynes: It lies among meadows through which wind the Ouzel and its tributary brooks, and has thatched cottages which must have looked for centuries much as they look today.*'

So says Arthur Mee in *Buckinghamshire*. Things have changed since then, Arthur. Milton Keynes is now a low, laid out landscape. Row upon row of units, domestic and industrial. It's tarmac and brick. There's a bypass on either side of you, always, and the air smells like a jar of pear drops. And rising from the middle of it all is the angular maze of glass and concrete which the designers have imaginatively christened Central Milton Keynes.

I followed a red-stained cycle path called Redway, through housing estates of various styles, some hacienda, some pagoda, some cardboard box. Everywhere were estate agents' boards and the sound of concrete mixers, and gardens being created rather than dug over. You got the feeling that someone had only come up with the idea of Milton Keynes a few days before. The signposts had all been vandalised and pointed in directions such as up, and I found myself on a road called V3 which took me onto H8 where I tucked myself in behind a truck from Safeways and eventually reached the supermarket complex and the civic centre.

An information officer was talking to a journalist, or someone taking notes anyway. He said: 'Milton Keynes offers everything for a family to grow up happily.'

'Grow up into what?' said the journalist not taking his eyes off his notepad.

'Into anything they want. Milton Keynes is the perfect blend of countryside and city.'

'Is that why you've got concrete cows?'

Concrete cows! I had to see the concrete cows!

That night I found a place to stay in a maisonette between roads V8 and H5. A three storied house, the top one to sleep in, the middle one to eat in and the bottom one to put the car in. There was no sign on the door that suggested accommodation, but I'd been told construction workers often stayed there when they came to put up a new housing estate. They were probably in and out in a weekend.

I knocked, a woman answered, holding a baby.

'I'd like a room, please,' I said. She looked down at my laden bicycle, and my Al's Garage sapphire blue pullover with the black fleck and she said: 'Construction worker, aren't you? Doesn't matter, I'm used to construction workers. You can stay as long as you don't mind the baby crying all night.'

My entertainment for the evening consisted of a search for a telephone in working order. I wanted to tell someone I was coming to see them. In days gone by I usually adopted the foot in the door approach: 'Hi, you don't know me but I'm a friend of Dave's, and Dave said if ever I was passing number twelve I should call in and ... '

'But this is number thirteen!'

'Not to worry, I'm not superstitious, just hungry ... ' and by that time, before they're able to hit you with some other lame excuse like: 'but I don't know anyone called Dave!' you've got your coat off, your luggage in the spare bedroom and you're sitting down at the table waiting to be fed. Those were more desperate times though, normally overseas, and I had innocence down to a fine art. Nowadays, I've come to realise that if you phone up the night before and perhaps turn up with a bottle of wine you might even get an invitation to call again.

I followed the walkways towards the city centre. Three kids were leaning out of their bedroom windows shouting across the piazza their plans for the evening. By the look of things though, what kids in Milton Keynes did most evenings was smash up telephone boxes. The first one I came across looked as though someone had lost their temper with a chain saw inside it. The second one had had its wires cut. I found a nest of kiosks outside Waitrose, but the first two were 999 calls only and the others were all vandalised apart from one that operated on a phone card.

I found another in a pub but I couldn't get a dialling tone. The one outside the extensive garden centre had had its receiver stuck down with Superglue. I joined a queue for the booth in the enormous cinema complex, but with three people to go before me the coin box jammed. Eventually I burst into a wine bar and demanded the house telephone. I dialled my number. There was no reply.

'It's impossible to be bored in Milton Keynes,' is another of the city's publicity by-lines. In which case I and a number of other people managed the impossible that night. Little cabals wandered across the shopping malls and sat around the indoor fountain. The city seemed enclosed like a space station and everyone remained within its four walls as if it was impossible to survive outside in the open air. I stood in front of a Radio Rentals window for a while and watched England close the first day's play at 248 for 5, but soon like everyone else I was drawn instinctively to the unit that generated the instantly recognizable red and yellow lights and logos, the familiar colours and smells of Macdonalds.

A favourite cartoon of mine shows a well-fed mogul sitting in an office with a bank of televisions before him, a fast food chain restaurant pictured on each screen. He speaks into a microphone: 'Shaftesbury Ave. Table six. Man sitting reading book.'

But that's why fast food restaurants work. You're in and out so quickly the eating process is desensitised. And so it was a surprise in Milton Keynes when I ordered a quarter pounder and fries and the assistant said: 'I'm sorry sir, it'll take three minutes. Will you sit down and wait?' A fatal mistake. Three minutes with nothing to do in a Macdonalds, I discovered, is precisely the length of time it takes the customer to realise he doesn't want to eat there.

Next morning at breakfast I was joined by a Scottish couple passing through on holiday. We sat at table reading the local papers.

I said, 'It says here that Simon Barnard of Stony Stratford was treated in Milton Keynes Hospital after a bicycle accident at the Thornborough Wadden crossroads.'

The Scotsman said, 'It says here that after a month long debate over the placing of a new bus shelter in Dunstable, the problem was solved when the council decided to put it on the site of the old one.'

I told him I was cycling and he told me he was a bus driver and his wife said how impressed she was with Milton Keynes. They lived in a similar sort of new town near Glasgow.

'Like here, each estate has a separate name and style,' he said.

'And like here, each estate has a communal spirit,' she said.

'And like here are all the telephone boxes vandalised?' I asked.

'We've all got phone cards,' he said.

That morning I bought myself a phonecard and then went to see the concrete cows. They were in a field, visible from the road, black and white sculptures that, according to the town guide, were famous the world over. They were refreshing to look at because they were the first sign that Milton Keynes had a sense of humour, that it didn't take itself so seriously after all. Maybe that was it, though: Milton Keynes was basically humourless. It was purpose built and it was predictable. It had no twists and turns. Every amenity, every newly planted sapling and every person had an allocated place and role. Milton Keynes needed a few more concrete cows.

Two days into the journey and I was becoming concerned about my physical state.

I wasn't aching anywhere. I had no blisters and no stiffness. No cuts, no bruises, no strains and no sprains. Surely by now I should have had at least a rupture. But no, for all this unaccustomed exercise my only physiological problem was an unnatural craving for bananas, itself a side-effect of a cycling trip to Holland I'd undertaken as a youth, a trip which saw a lifelong loathing of the curved yellow fruit replaced by an addiction. Bananas were cheap, really cheap.

I had little money, really little money. I ate bananas by the bunch and since then I can't ride a bicycle without wanting to eat a banana and vice versa.

On the mechanical front, though, my gears were still giving me grief. I had to admit I was confused. Each time I stripped down the derailleur, adjusted it then put it back together again I was left with a nut or a washer or some strange shape spare. My pocket rattled with redundant pivots, bolts, locknuts and jockey rollers, and yet, the gears were definitely performing better. I now had six out of ten. Maybe they were defunct organs I was discarding, the bicycle's equivalent of the appendix.

The Test Match was growing more interesting. England were all out for 307. New Zealand had begun their innings and had quickly lost their first 2 wickets for 5 runs when suddenly, the Queen arrived. A brilliant piece of tactical play by England, and Brian Johnson interrupted his ball by ball commentary of the match to give a stitch by stitch account of the Queen's dress.

They took tea, and my day slipped into a wispy-skied, cool summer's evening, thick with the smell of cut grass and burning compost, and I was cycling through red-bricked Northamptonshire villages and then along a gated road towards the setting sun.

Setting sun!? Heading in that sort of direction had the feel of a westerly rather than a northerly motion to it. But so what, I had all summer, and if I was going to Lapland I was going to go the pretty way. I wanted to follow any road I liked the look of and stop anywhere I fancied stopping. The village of Badby was just such a place. I stayed at a pub with an American couple, a German couple and an English couple. The English couple tried to talk to the Germans in German. The Germans tried to talk to the Americans in English. The Americans just talked.

They'd only arrived in the village two hours previously

but they already knew the history of the place from the time of the Norman Conquest. They knew the village postman, the 'Bobby', the little old lady out there painting her gate, the man with the size eleven feet sitting on the green reading the evening newspaper, and of course the vicar who had given them a tour of the church and put them on his Christmas card list.

We all sat there watching the cricket highlights on BBC2.

'Explain cricket,' said the German woman to me. She had a St Michael's jersey on with the label sticking out of the back.

'Well ... it's not quite as easy as that,' I said. 'Cricket is a game where a lot more than rules apply. It's a mental as well as a physical contest, requiring a philosophical ... '

'Cricket is very simple, really,' said the American, 'there are two sides; they take it in turns to bat and then to bowl, and the side that scores the most, wins. Simple ... '

'But ... '

'What does the Queen do?' said the Germans, when HRH arrived.

'The Queen loves cricket,' said the American woman.

'And tennis,' said the German lady.

The Americans had just been to Stratford-on-Avon: 'Even the banks have Tudor timbers there,' they said. But it was Ann Hathaway's cottage that had made the greatest impression on them: 'Did you know that Ann Hathaway used to bathe only once every two weeks?'

The Germans rallied with: 'Did you know that Mary Queen of Scots was over six foot tall and an excellent billiards player?'

The Americans came back with: 'I discovered the other day that Isambard Kingdom Brunel used to wear his top hat in bed.'

'Did you know the Lapps are the shortest race in Europe?' I chipped in.

But the one thing both parties were agreed upon was that England didn't let the visitor down and the English behaved just as you expected them to: they were sentimental and eccentric; they were easily embarrassed and they all had gnomes holding fishing rods stuck in their gardens. But then these tourists were all following the same uncontaminated route through the English shires, travelling mostly on coach trips, in glass bubbles that set off from underground car parks in London each morning at six a.m. and rolled along on well worn rails around the Stonehenge-Warwick Castle-Stratford-on-Avon circuit, managing to convince all on board that England is a nation of tradesmen and aristocracy who come home to their castles each evening to eat a banquet, do a bit of Morris dancing, recite some Shakespeare and then curl up in a four poster. It's difficult to explain to this kind of visitor that as their coaches speed back to their Knightsbridge hotels, your average Englishman is sitting at home with his Pot Noodles watching the Two Ronnies on the video.

Although, on that particular night in Badby, they should have got the general idea, as the local dilettantes drove through the village in a souped-up Morris Marina doing wheelies and hand brake turns around the green. I lay in bed wondering where the Bobby was that the Americans had got on with so famously. The Morris stopped outside the pub. Stones started to hit my window. I heard some giggles and a rapping of knuckles on the glass. Just Friday night high spirits I thought, and turned over. Then I remembered I was on the first floor. I whipped back the curtains to see a gormless face frosted with beer, staring at me. The lad was clinging to the drainpipe, knuckles poised. I tugged the window open and said:

'*Finnes det en skøyte-bane i naerheten?*'
which I thought meant:
'I want to go to sleep.'

But in fact means:
'Is there a skating-rink near here?'

It was the night a disused sports pavilion in Warwick caught fire and was slightly damaged; the night a Ford Sierra driven by a Mr H. Yeats of Solihull hit a curry house in Coventry and no-one was hurt; the night a pensioner from West Bromwich completed his first week of non-stop hiccoughing.

I was sitting on Badby village green listening to local radio and searching for gear number seven:

'Hang on to chain roller cage to prevent spinning and remove cage stop bolt SB. Let unwind and then remove pivot bolt B. Slide out pivot bolt A and adjoining spring. Back off high gear adjusting screw E to minimise changer body spring tension and undo spring bolt SS. Screw in spring bolt SS. Replace cage spring and slide in pivot bolt. Replace jockey roller and stop bolt, tension roller and cable.' Fine. I can understand all that. What I can't understand is the spare metal object in my hand. It could be a pivot bolt B, a cage bolt C or a superfluous bolt S.

I put it in my pocket P with all the others, then continued westwards along lanes into Warwickshire; seven gears working, only three more to find; New Zealand beginning to recover from the disastrous start to their innings; and I'd decided to visit Stratford-on-Avon myself and see first hand this Mecca to which every excursion coach is instinctively drawn.

Also on the road to Stratford that day was Oliver, a tramp, a true gentleman of the road with all the qualifications: he smelt, he had a shabby coat, a frayed tie, thin legs and a pot belly. He was a tramp's tramp, the only discrepancy in his appearance being a rolled up tent strapped to his back. I walked along next to him, pushing my bike.

'I don't like your pullover!' he said.

Oliver was on his way to Worcester to pick up his new army pension book. He could have had it posted to the nearest DHSS office, but: 'I don't like being a burden on the postal service. I'll walk there and pick it up myself.'

He asked me where I was headed and when I told him Newcastle, he said: 'Up through Stratford on to Worcester, Ludlow, Shrewsbury, Whitchurch, Chester, Stockport, over the Cat and Fiddle, Manchester ... '

He knew every route from anywhere to everywhere. The trouble was once he started he couldn't stop. He was like a tramp on the Circle Line, except his journey was an annual one and took him right around the country. His life was caught on rails; he had no brakes and no way of stepping off.

'Where are you going after you pick up your pension?' I asked.

'Oh, up to Leominster, Shrewsbury, Oswestry, Nantwich, St. Helens, Burnley, Lancaster, Kendall ... ' he needed to be slapped if he was going to stop. He was like the pensioner in West Bromwich with incurable hiccoughs. A Ford Sierra turned off the B4086 to Alveston almost running Oliver over and gave him the shock he needed. When he'd recovered he asked me where I came from.

'St. Albans,' I said and immediately wished I hadn't.

'Ah, St. Albans, Hemel, Kings Langley, Berkhamstead, Tring, Aylesbury, Kingswood, Bicester ... '

He hesitated momentarily on Bicester and I managed to distract him with an apple.

'Life's all right as long as you've got a bit of grub,' he said and began to shine what was a perfectly clean apple on his perfectly mucky jacket.

'Where do you normally get your grub from?' I asked

'I can always find work if I want. You wouldn't catch me in an office though. I couldn't work in a firm of solicitors, for instance. It would drive me crazy. I work on farms mostly, fruit picking. Or with pigs. Pigs are nice to work with. Pigs won't hurt you. I can work anywhere. I got my tent you see. You got a tent?'

'No, I want to get one.'

'Get yourself one of these. It's a good one. Cost hundred pounds new. I got it cheap.'

'How much?'

'Nothing. Good buy if you ask me. 'Course it's full of holes. Don't matter though, I spread it down on the ground and lie on top of it. Getting a bit old for camping holidays now though. My health has gone for a burton, Swadlincote, Coalville, Leicester, Uppingham, Peterborough, Wisbech ... ' His face was beginning to go red. He wasn't breathing as he spoke: ' ... Kings Lynn, East Dereham, Norwich ... '

'Great Yarmouth!'

'Great Yarmouth.' He'd reached the sea and could go no further.

We kept on walking, never stopping or even altering pace for two hours. In mid afternoon we reached the 'Welcome to Stratford-on-Avon' signpost.

'Don't like big places,' said Oliver, 'I used to live in London but there were too many tramps for my liking. I lived in Kilburn, then Cricklewood, Hendon, Mill Hill, Elstree, Radlett, Watford ... '

'I'm stopping here,' I said when we got into the town centre. But Oliver just kept on walking: ' ... Luton, Bedford, Rushden, Kettering, Stamford ... ' his voice fading as he shuffled along, shoulders hunched, heading steadily for the North of Scotland.

A summer's Saturday, and Stratford was a mixture of diesel fumes and ice creams, the click of Kodachrome and the Test Match commentary. A minstrel dressed up as Henry VIII stood outside the Royal Shakespeare Theatre and busked on a lute, playing songs from the Tudor hit parade. Maverick troops of Morris Dancers roamed the open spaces making it difficult to sit down on the grass without being trampled on.

I joined a group of Japanese tourists as they were led round Shakespeare's Birthplace by an official tourist board robot. They were all dressed in black raincoats, and assiduously searched in every cupboard and under every bed, looking for what I don't know, mislaid manuscripts perhaps, *Hamlet Strikes Back* or *Three Gentlemen of Verona*. Although, it soon became clear that these weren't Shakespeare enthusiasts so much as groupies, all their questions seemed far more concerned with what the immortal bard had for breakfast than with anything he ever wrote. One of them had a To Be Or Not To Be t-shirt!

Outside, however, as they lined up to take photographs, they revealed their true identities. And it turned out that these weren't just any visitors from Japan. They were a crack troop of specially trained kamikaze tourists.

The best view of Shakespeare's House is undoubtedly the one to be had gazing upwards whilst standing in the road outside. Unfortunately, while this road may well have been a quiet back street when our William was a lad, it's now the main thoroughfare for coaches making for the Shakespeare's House Car Park and the scene is one of mayhem as little Orientals, cameras in hand, try to dodge twenty ton lumps of Mercedes. 'Is more honourable to end up impaled on Grey Green Coach Company radiator grill than return home without picture of self outside Shakespeare's House.' As it is most Japanese back home now imagine Shakespeare was born on a bus.

I bought a table mat with the Complete Works on as a souvenir and, clutching my phonecard, went in search of a phone box. The only ones I could find were coin operated. The first one was smashed to bits. The second was jammed. The third had a queue about as long as the one for *A Midsummer Night's Dream*. Eventually I found one a few miles out of town. Inside was a fourteen-year-old girl. I know her age because the first thing I heard was:

'But I'm fourteen, honestly.' She spoke with a cracked, pleading voice. 'I am ... why not? ... you promised you would ... but you said you didn't mind ... why not tonight? ... it's not my fault ... I didn't lose it, it fell off ... why not? ... why? ... '.

Her voice trailed away. She looked at the phone for a moment and then slammed it back on the bracket. My first thought was: if she's broken the bloody thing I'll make a citizen's arrest on her! But as she turned I could see she had tears running down her face. She brushed past me clutching her money.

I tried my friend again. She lived in the nearby village of Kineton. I dialled, the number rang, someone answered and the money slipped in, and I felt a rush of achievement at my first successful phone call of the trip.

'Hello, is that Sandra? ... it's Mark. I was just passing through your area and I thought I'd ... Mark, Mark Wallington ... yes, I was just passing through quite near to your village and I thought I'd ... what? ... Mark Wallington. I'm a friend of Joanna's, we met a few months ago, remember ... yes ... anyway, I'm just down the road from Kineton and I thought why not give Sandra a call and ... you must remember ... we all went to a Greek restaurant ... yes that's right ... well Joanna gave me your address and ... no you didn't share a mese with me, I think you shared one with Douglas ... what? ... Douglas? Oh Douglas is fine ... yes, he is a nice guy isn't he? ... anyway I was passing on my bicycle and ... that's right I was the one who spilt the glass of retsina over you ... yes ... anyway Joanna said why not look up Sandra if you're nearby ... pardon? ... completely ruined the dress, eh? ... '

She took pity on me. I found her cottage and she immediately bundled me into her car and took me to

Edgehill to watch the sunset. We sat in the garden of the pub on the hilltop overlooking the battleground where in 1642 Charles the First and the Royalist troops, marching towards London, came across the Parliamentarians under Robert Devereux, Earl of Essex, in the first major confrontation of the Civil War. Among the Royalists that day was Sir Jacob Astley. Before the battle began he prayed: 'Lord, thou knowest how busy I shall be this day. If I forget thee, do not thou forget me.' I remember the prayer well. It hung above the sink in my mother's kitchen every day of my childhood. Now I stood on the hilltop and gazed down into the valley and closed my eyes and tried to picture the battle, but all I could visualise was piles of dirty dishes.

'Used to be all so very different years ago ... ' said the man sitting next to us, sucking an unlit pipe, ' ... when the elms were alive ... and the hedgerows were all over ... before they changed things ... before they cleared half the beeches from the hill ... ' He rocked and nodded. ' ... You couldn't see a damn thing then.'

We went inside. A woman came in with a long thin animal on a lead. It was a polecat crossed with a ferret, she said.

'Best pet I ever had. It won't hurt unless it bites or scratches you. Name's Sandy. She was such a comfort to my mother when she was dying of cancer. By the way do you want to buy a raffle ticket for a fridge freezer?'

'Lots of strange people round here,' said Sandra. She'd done what few country people could understand a single woman doing. She'd moved out from the city into the sticks instead of vice versa. 'Everyone thinks I've got a past,' she said.

But since she did have a past this was very observant of them. She'd travelled; she'd been on television with Rod Hull and his emu; she had a microwave oven; she'd once lived in a flat on the floor above Russ Conway. She thought moving out from London would be settling but she was getting itchy feet again.

'Are you really going to cycle all the way to Lapland?' she said on Sunday afternoon. We were in a Pick Your Own fruit and vegetable plantation. Somewhere amongst the two hundred acres of raspberries, gooseberries and courgettes was the broad bean field we were looking for.

'Yes, I'm going to Lapland.'

'Why?'

'Raising money for charity.'

'What charity?'

'Er ... Band Aid. Feed the World.'

'You get good reindeer hatstands in Lapland, you know.'

'Yes, I know.'

'I'd love to pack up and go off again.'

I was slowly coming to terms with travelling on my own. To begin with I'd thought about asking someone to come with me on this trip, Kate Bush had been top of my list, but ultimately a journey of this nature has to be done solo. I was travelling in the hope of the unexpected happening to me. I wanted to experience the peculiar and the eccentric, and being on my own I was more vulnerable. Not to danger – I never feel in danger when travelling in England; no matter were I go I know I'm never far from a town, a telephone or a bus stop – but vulnerable to the situations that rarely arise when you're travelling in company. And I wanted these experiences for myself. Travel like this was selfish and sometimes lonesome, but it was the only way to go.

'Why not come with me then?' I said.

But she decided not to, didn't give it a thought, it never crossed her mind in fact, not for one moment did she seriously consider the matter. Instead, the next morning she gave me some tuna fish sandwiches wrapped in silver foil to take along as company.

It was Monday. A man had been arrested in connection

with the Stockwell Stranglings. Greg Lemond of the USA won the Tour de France. I was sitting on the pavement outside Sandra's cottage feeling pleased with myself. I'd just stripped down, readjusted and reassembled my alternator cage so it was now the recommended half inch above the front sprocket, enabling me to find my eighth gear.

'What's this bit on the ground,' said Sandra, picking up what could have been a mounting bolt B or a locking bolt C.

I showed her the rest. 'What shall I do with them all?' I said.

'Throw them away,' said Sandra.

No, I couldn't do that. That was ridiculous.

'I'd like a *kahte*, please.' I said to the assistant in Milletts.

'A what?'

'A *kahte*. Or failing that a *goatti*.'

I was of course referring to the classic Lapp nomad's tent, an easily transported forked pole construction similar to the wigwam or teepee of the North American Indian. It takes about half an hour to erect and is carried along with the birch twigs needed for the floor on the last sledge of the train. There are adjustable door flaps, and a provision for a smoke hole.

'Sorry mate, this is Milletts,' he said.

But one look round the array of canvas in the showroom made me realise I didn't want a camping holiday. It was the rigmarole of it all I detested, and the very thought of sitting in a tent each night made me feel isolated. It wasn't as if I needed anything elaborate. Despite its northerly latitudes, my information told me the Lapland summers often vied with the Mediterranean as the warmest in Europe.

'Listen, what I want is something compact, waterproof, easy to carry, lightweight and inconspicuous.'

'Er ... we've got this,' he said, and with the sort of flourish you don't normally expect from Milletts' staff he presented

me with a six berth touring tent with a chemical lavatory, a
patio and surrounding fence with gate. Kennel optional.

It began to rain heavily as I passed through the Swine
Fever infected area of Astwood Bank. I took shelter under a
bridge and took solace in Sandra's sandwiches. Rain had
stopped play at the Test Match, a draw was looking more
and more likely. On Wyvern local radio the big news of the
day concerned the police accident prevention vehicle that
had rolled over on the motorway and caused a four hour hold
up. I tried listening to the Commonwealth Games from
Edinburgh but God! have you ever considered how boring
swimming is on the radio? I tuned to a music station which
announced a song called 'Lady in Red' by Chris de Burgh had
just reached number one. It was the theme of the summer,
lightweight but well-made, adjectives that could also
describe Sandra's tuna fish sandwiches. I took the last one. A
lone truck passed. On the windscreen was a sticker that read:
'Lose weight now, ask me how.' The driver hooted and
splashed me with a puddle, making my sandwich soggy and
muddy and inedible. If that was how he proposed losing
weight he could count me out.

The River Severn was swollen and agitated as I battled
against the wind over its bridge. But you see nothing cycling
in weather like this. Nothing but road signs. Droitwich 3
miles, said one ahead of me, which was annoying because a
mile back I could have sworn I'd past one saying Droitwich
2½ miles. On a bicycle signs like this can really upset you.
Much more fun are the signs and notices stuck on village
bulletin boards. Every village had one and they were like
little soap-operas. On display there'd be a bus timetable to
the nearest market town; a What's On at the local youth
club; the day and time of the next weight watchers class.
There'd be an advert for a mobile disco usually called Dave's
or Derek's Disco; notification of an Alms House up for rent
to local person only; where the local bottle bank was

situated; the time of the local M.P.'s next surgery; the team
sheet for the next cricket fixture; the next W.I. meeting; on
a post nearby or stuck on some railings there'd always be a
lone glove or scarf waiting to be claimed; and of course
there'd be a number of cards stuck up: 'Washing machine for
sale, very little use.' On one board I remember seeing a card
saying 'Man wants work. Will do anything,' and next to it
another: 'Wanted: a man who will do anything.' I would
have put them in touch with each other but the local
telephone box was jammed.

Late that afternoon I reached the Teme valley. A lush and
vivid green landscape of hills and hedges. The basin was
saturated with the swollen river. The road was like a mirror.

With my eight gears working admirably I climbed to the
villages called the Shelseys and from there you could see for
miles. In the distance there were mountains, sharp and dark
and which I presumed to be in Wales. But visibility faded as
the rain grew heavy. I sheltered under a tree by a lone house,
and read a sodden newspaper I'd found in the gutter: June 25,
Wimbledon fortnight well underway, Pat Cash putting on a
brave display to reach the Quarter Finals. That heat hazed
week seemed years away now.

In the house a hand wiped a hole in a window of
condensation and a face stared out. I waved. A dog barked
and a doberman came bounding out and chased me away.

The light was failing, the rain was succeeding. In the
distance I could see a woman walking down the road herding
sheep. I stopped her and asked if she knew somewhere
nearby to stay. She turned out to be Austrian. The village of
Hippach in the Zillertal she knew like the back of her hand
but concerning the Teme Valley she was less knowledgable.

'Did you vatch the royal wedding?' she said.

'Yes. No-one puts on a show of pageantry like the British,
do they?'

'No. We foreigners are a bit jealous of your royal family, you know.'

I followed the river downstream and eventually found a farmhouse to put me up and dry me out. The farmer's wife was a most industrious woman, making jam with one hand, feeding the pigs with the other. And ten piglets were born that night as the rain rattled my window and windfalls bombarded the orchards. The next morning she led me through the waterlogged yard to see the new born. The bloated and exhausted mother lay there supine, her little pink mites searching blindly for nipples, the whole family kept warm by electric lights.

'Pigs are good to work with,' said the farmer's wife, substantiating Oliver's theory. 'We'll fatten this litter, keep them for a year or so, and then kill 'em. Tell you what, come and have a look at the new Mitsubishi four wheel drive.'

I sent a postcard to Ralph: 'One week into trip. Everything going remarkably well. Thanks for putting me up. It was me that ate the Sainsbury's cheese and bacon flan.'

And things were going well. I'd have to check this annoying tendency to head west rather than north, and I was travelling a bit slowly perhaps, but it would have been wrong to hurry off at this stage. Besides wanting this section of the journey to be a gradual build-up to peak condition, it was also a chance, I kept reminding myself, to see parts of England I'd never seen before. The Teme Valley for example; it was beautiful and I'd never even heard of it. In fact, the whole of Worcestershire I'd never taken the time to get to know. Nor Shropshire, the county I was heading into. They both seemed to be so easily bypassed. Their only motorway clung to their eastern borders. Conurbations of any size were few. And from here North, as my mental map of England began to blur, I had little idea of what to expect. Before I left I'd been just as excited about seeing the North

of England properly for the first time, as seeing the North
Cape. Friends from the North who had settled in the South
East had convinced me I was an archetypal product of the
South, the sort who thinks the North is all cloth caps and
brass bands, Coronation Street and Hovis; that area of
England purposely left out on a cultural limb, where back
doors are open all day, and the nation's heritage is on public
display. And Northerners, of course, are unemployed but
happy, proud even of their poverty. They're unfashionable
and poorly informed, yet stubborn and opinionated, and
their opinion of Southerners is simply that they're opportu-
nists who don't know they're born.

This sort of impression, apparently, makes it clear I've
never really spent any time North of the television set. As it
was, I was already beginning to sense a change. I wasn't in
the north of the country yet, not by a long way, but after
Stratford-on-Avon I'd begun to feel myself draw free from
the gravitational pull of London, which plucked commuters
from villages as far north as Coventry. The accents were
sharpening. People were beginning to call me Duck.
Parochialisms were emerging. People wanted to know what
I was doing wearing a pullover like that in their village and
how much I'd paid for my bike. Travelling at the pace I was,
I was passing through the country in slow motion, and this
was making me feel more and more like an homogenised
product of the South East.

I followed the river Teme once more, into Tenbury
Wells, a market town which couldn't cope with its market
traffic. A van forced me into the curb and clipped the blinds
of a men's outfitters. I decided to walk and came eventually
to the market hall, a rotund, crumbling cake of a building.
Inside, flowers and vegetables were being auctioned, but in
such small quantities it seemed pointless.

'What am I bid for this bunch of spring onions?' shouted
the diminutive auctioneer, standing on tip toes and holding

up what was undeniably a bunch of spring onions, about ten of them. 'Do I hear 20 pence? 20 pence, 25 pence. Sold to Mrs Goole for 25p. How's your leg by the way Mrs Goole? Better? Good. Now. Dahlias. Twopence each or a bunch for 15p. Look very nice in your hallway they would Mrs McGuinness.'

More interesting was the W.I. market across the road, stuffed with homemade produce. And yet, whereas in supermarkets any products with homemade pretensions are exhibited on a farmyard display counter, packaged in a box with a Constable print on the cover and given names like Mrs Woodcote's Country Style, in the Tenbury W.I. market, where the stock really did come straight from the members' kitchens, probably baked the night before, they were trying to extol its virtues as convenience food, the sort you could buy in any reputable chain store. As you walked in you were handed a little wire basket. All the produce was stamped with a price gun and stacked in displays. Sponge cakes were packed in boxes with a Best Before date. Even the helpers had little checked tunics. I bought a gooseberry pie which a woman placed on a foil tray and then tried to put in a plastic bag, one of those you find by supermarket vegetable counters, the ones you rip off a roll and then spend the next half hour trying to discover how to open. She fiddled with it, pinched it, rubbed it, licked it, then finally blew it open, slipped the pie inside and stapled it up.

The smell of the jam factory followed me as I headed out of town towards Ludlow. The last day of the Test Match was under way and Graham Gooch was heading for his seventh Test century, but the game was petering out to an inevitable draw. The players took lunch at one o'clock; so did I.

Like Stratford-on-Avon, Ludlow is a town in black-and-white stripes, its centre a marriage of medieval and Boots the Chemist. The Feathers Hotel is the model to which all other buildings aspire. As pretty as a jigsaw and fragile as a house of cards, like all buildings of architectural interest in the town, it has its history embossed on a blue plaque and stuck up on a wall by members of the Ludlow Civic society. You see these plaques everywhere you walk in Ludlow: 'This house was destroyed by fire in the Civil War, then rebuilt.' 'The blacksmith lived here.' 'The farrier lived here.' 'The man who worked behind the counter down the fishmongers on a Thursday afternoon when Mr Thomson, the manager, had his day off, lived here.'

The truth is, so ubiquitous are these awards that they cease to attract the attention. You expect to see plaques like 'First house in Ludlow to be awarded a blue plaque'. It's the houses without recognition that catch the eye instead. You stop and gaze at a Bovis semi and think: I wonder why that house hasn't got a blue plaque?

As it was, the highlight of my short visit to Ludlow was undoubtedly the enormous French bread roll I had in the Castle Cafe. Building on Ludlow Castle commenced in 1085 undertaken by the powerful Marcher Lord Roger Montgomery. Surrounded by woodland and a natural cliff bastion overlooking the River Teme, the castle was a vital stronghold, and fortification continued until the Fifteenth Century. There are substantial remains. The construction of my French bread roll was undertaken earlier that morning by the woman with the national health glasses who works in the Castle Cafe kitchen. It had a fresh crisp base and was fortified by cheese, lettuce, tomato and Branston pickle. I began eating it at 1.15 p.m. and continued until completion at 1.32 p.m. There are no remains whatsoever.

I walked around the gridded streets of the town, standing under awnings to avoid the showers. Pressed up against an estate agents' window I stood next to two girls who couldn't believe their eyes at the property prices. When they saw the timbered, three bedroomed cottage with the thatched roof they clasped each other and slipped into hysteria.

'Just look at the price of that,' said the one who looked like the woman who sometimes reads the Six o'Clock News. 'I could sell my one bedroomed flat in Dulwich, buy that and still have five thousand left over for the extension to the kitchen that's obviously needed.'

Her friend, who had already made the move from London, said: 'You'll never regret it. Best move I ever made, coming to Ludlow. There's even a castle, look.' She pointed towards the castle and her friend looked and thought: I could probably afford it but the restoration work would be extensive.

'The best move I ever made,' was the most common phrase I heard in Ludlow. And you could see the attraction of the area; it seemed ludicrously cheap. Even the second-hand bicycles advertised in the newsagents' windows were bargains. But then there were also advertisements for jobbing gardeners, offering wages of £2 an hour. I was earning £4 in London when I did the same job five years ago.

It was in the castle grounds, when I leant my bike against a tree and turned round to hear it crash onto the gravel, that I gained my last two gears. I picked the bike up and found the derailleur slipped from one to ten, from large sprocket to big sprocket and back again, with well-oiled ease. I was just about to cycle off when a couple stopped and the man said 'You dropped this,' and he handed me what looked like a bolt G. 'Thanks,' I said, and slipped it into my pocket.

'Just passing through?' he asked. I said I was, and he stood back to admire my bike which, covered in the mud and oil of a week's weather, looked, I thought, suitably unadmirable. He had all the body language of a cycling freak – the stroking of the chin and the nods and aha!s of a man who can talk for an hour about mudguard sizes. I thought I was going to get one of those 'are you using 24 inch or 26 inch tyres? 'cos if you're using 26 inch you'll have a hell of a time in Shropshire,' sort of conversations. But instead he said:

'You'll like Shropshire. Best move we ever made coming to live here. I work for the Gas, see. I can work anywhere. We came to Oswestry and bought a three bedroomed detached.'

'Life is so much slower here,' said his wife.

'Slower attractive or slower boring?' I asked.

'Slower attractive, definitely,' she said.

'Definitely,' he said.

The man suggested I look them up in their three bedroomed detached if I was going anywhere near Oswestry. I jumped at the chance as usual.

'Might be a bit difficult though,' I said, 'I don't have you address. Ha.'

'No, of course he doesn't,' said the woman and pulled her husband away.

Before I left I went into a camping shop and explained how I was going to the Arctic Circle, how I didn't want a tent, and how my plans for the evenings ahead were to spend most of the time in convivial company practising my Norwegian and then if no-one had offered me shelter by midnight just to crash out under the stars wrapped up in something waterproof, Oliver-style.

'Got just the thing for someone who wants to spend most of his time in convivial company and then if no-one has offered him shelter, to crash out under the stars wrapped up in something waterproof,' said the assistant and he produced a package called a Gore-Tex bivibag.

'Engineered protection, this,' he said, quoting from the label. 'It's as waterproof as urethane coated fabrics and yet as permeable to perspiration vapour as polycotton cloth.'

'How much?'

'Even the seams have been factory sealed.'

'How much?'

'Each square inch has got nine million pores.'

'How much?'

'Seventy quid. That's cheap for nine million of something.'

It was perfect. I could sleep anywhere in this, and it would fit in my pocket.

'I'll take it,' I said.

'The unique combination of properties permit many functions to be combined in a single garment.'

'Yes, all right. I'll take it.'

'You see, the key to the fabric is in the microporous Gore-Tex film which is laminated between the inner and outer layers.'

'Okay. You've convinced me.'

'So you're protected from external moisture while internal body vapour is allowed to escape from within.'

'Give it to me, will you?'

I snatched it off him, paid him and cycled out of town. At five o'clock the Test Match was announced a draw. The rain was the culprit, and although it had now stopped and a watery evening sun bathed amongst the clouds, the sky looked bleak and the pictures of the royal wedding lying in the roadside wouldn't have time to dry.

I stopped in a layby. The weight from the assortment of pivot bolts P and washers C and G in my trouser pocket was now considerable. I took them out and looked at them, then after a moment's deliberation threw them into a litter bin and headed off towards the hills I could see in the distance. They were hunch-backed and deep green, but more significantly, they were directly north.

3. Derbyshire: Back Axle

An evening ride through the Long Mynd, the ten mile range of bleak and bare hills that forms the last English barrier before Wales; 1700 feet at their highest point and surely fashioned by moles.

Mynd is Welsh for mountain and the area is known locally as Little Switzerland, so when I came across Burway Hill just outside Church Stretton, and saw a sign warning of a five in one gradient ahead, I thought: just the job to test myself.

The journey up through Norway was going to be tough, I realised that. More than a thousand miles of fjord. A road that twisted and turned, climbed and fell, thousands of feet at a time. A road broken by winter frosts, and winding through long stretches of uninhabited country, becoming wilder and more remote the further north I went. Or at least this was the impression I'd got from my local travel agent when I asked for information on Lapland and was given a brochure with a picture of a blonde girl holding a fish in front of her face on the cover. Mind you, the photographs inside also gave the impression that every man in Scandinavia was bald.

I stood up on the pedals and set off, the narrow road disappearing into the hillside helter skelter style, and so steep my panniers began to slip. After fifty yards there was a loud crack from the back wheel. After a hundred yards there was a loud crack from my left ankle. After a hundred and two yards I got off and walked.

In fact walking is the best way to ascend hills as beautiful as these. From the top of Burway I could see the whole range. They were treeless, round shouldered beasts that crouched on the land like prone dogs, the thin vegetation barely covering their frame. You could see the bones in these hills.

This was the first really dramatic landscape I'd come across and such scenery always stops you in your tracks. You stand there and try to take it all in, to remember that peak, that woodland, that valley, and then as soon as you turn away the picture begins to blur, and you keep looking back trying to imprint it on your memory, knowing that no matter what promises you make yourself, it's unlikely you'll ever return to this spot, and certainly not on a bicycle, at this age, or in this frame of mind.

And so just passing through a landscape becomes generally unsatisfactory. Scenery needs to be lived in, to be seen in all seasons and in all weathers to be properly appreciated. You can't really understand it until you've worked it, been lost in it, fought against it in a snowstorm or laid down on it in the sunshine with someone you love. Then does scenery become vivid rather than merely a backdrop. I felt I wanted to show the Long Mynd to someone, someone who I knew would appreciate it. To say: 'Look, I've found this place. I really like it and I thought you'd really like it too. Look at the colour of that wood. Look at the clouds just charging in from Wales. I bet it's wonderful in the winter here as well.'

Mr and Mrs Hollins put me up in their caravan that night. It stood next to their house, sharing a field with a few sheep. The Hollinses had wanted, I'm sure, to invite me to stay in the house, but the English have always been peculiar about letting strangers into their homes. And I mean peculiar, not fearful. They're not frightened the stranger will rob or harm them, they're frightened he won't like the furniture, frightened he won't like the conversation and they'll be embarrassing silences. Over the last few days I'd quickly slipped into the talk-to-anyone, try-everything, put-anything-into-your-mouth mentality that all travellers sooner or later adopt. I wanted to trust people and to put them instantly at ease, and it was so frustrating to be out in the caravan while everyone else was inside watching the Commonwealth Games and eating biscuits.

In the morning, though, the Hollinses called to me to come inside for breakfast. I think they felt sorry for me. All night rain had fallen on the caravan roof like gravel and now the hills had vanished in a thick mist.

'Where are you headed?' asked Mr Hollins.

'Lapland,' I said.

'Lapland eh? You'll want the Shrewsbury road, then. Your back axle's on the way out, by the way,' and he picked up my bike and shook it and it rattled. 'What you want to do is undo locknut A from cone B. Hold the axle housing with a wrench at locknut C. Screw cone B fully and then back off with a quarter turn, slide in new axle G and reverse the process. Easy enough job.'

Yes, and if I attempted it, I'd end up throwing ninety percent of the bike into layby litterbins.

I had scrambled egg in the warm, steamy kitchen. Like every room in the house it was full of boxes of homemade chutney, home fermented wine, potting trays and mustard and cress on blotting paper.

'Most people spend their time round here just nattering,' said Mrs Hollins, 'least, we do,' and she gave me an update on all the gossip in the valley since the Romans left, ending with the story of Charlie, the man who lived in the Bottom, and had never been out of the valley in his life. The BBC had made a television programme on the strength of his achievement.

I couldn't find any enthusiasm for cycling in the rain so I went into the local town, Bishop's Castle, with the Hollinses in their Landrover. Mr Hollins parked in the middle of the main street in Bishop's Castle. 'You can't do that in Piccadilly Circus can you?' he said, climbing out.

'No, you can't,' I said, although judging by the queue building up behind us and by the immediate blast of horns and abuse emanating from it, parking in the middle of the High Street wasn't something you could do in Bishop's Castle either.

Mr Hollins walked me round the town as if he were a guide, and everything he pointed out, – things like the farm shop, the DIY discount store and the DHSS building – he'd say: 'Bet you don't find anything like that in Piccadilly Circus?'

But the man's forte, his specialist subject, was the history of electrical shops in Bishop's Castle, 1948 to the present day. 'See that drapers?' he'd say, 'used to be an electrical shop. I worked there until it went bust in '56. See that chemist? That used to be an electricians'. Good little sparks that was. Went bust in '78 a few years after I started there.'

All the places where the poor man had worked had gone bust eventually. He'd been unemployed for four years now and he strolled aimlessly around town nodding a greeting to every other person he saw and stopping to chat with every fifth. The conversation invariably went thus:

'Cyril.'

'Ray.'

'All right?'

'Can't complain. Yourself?'

'Fair to Middlin.'

'Better than last week?'

'Oh aye, better than last week … Not as good as the week before though.'

'Worse than at Christmas?'

'No, not as bad as at Christmas.'

''Bout the same as the third week in March?'

'Yeah. 'Bout the same as the third week in March, I'd say.'

'See yer then Cyril.'

'See yer Ray.'

My tour of Bishop's Castle ended at the new public
conveniences in the cattle market, which Mr Hollins had
proudly saved until last. He drove round there especially,
parked the Landrover outside, told Mrs Hollins we wouldn't
be a minute then led me inside.

We stood at the urinals, side by side, gazing at the
tilework, backs arched, feet apart, heads up. I was trying to
think of something to say but Mr Hollins beat me to it:

'Plush eh? Bet you don't find anything like this in
Piccadilly Circus?'

Owing to its vast areas of stagnant water and its undersoil
heating from summer moss, Lapland provides ideal breeding
conditions for a particularly vicious species of mosquito. I'd
need to get some effective repellent sooner or later, but for
the time being I was learning to deal with insects in my own
way i.e. if any came near me I swallowed them. In fact so
many insects was I consuming, I fancied I was now able to
differentiate between the tastes. Butterflies were crunchy
and a good main meal; greenfly were nice on a salad;
Ladybirds were a tasty mid-morning snack. On one occasion
a midge travelling at approximately 15 miles an hour entered
my mouth as I was pedalling at about 10, hitting the back of
my throat at a combined speed of 25 m.p.h. Now that's what
I call fast food!

It was a wet and windy Wednesday, the last in July, and
Mark Wallington, fork-lift driver at Maynard and Packer
meat importers earning £140 a week plus luncheon vouchers,
was cycling through the Shropshire village of Cardington,
ahead of him a hill the size of K2.

I'd decided to add a bit of variety to the journey by
changing my identity. In Bishop's Castle the Hollinses had
assumed I was a teacher. But everyone assumed I was a

teacher, which was all right to begin with, but working in education quickly became uninspiring. If I was going to have a secret identity, I wanted to be someone enigmatic, someone with a dark and dubious background. A fork-lift driver was perfect.

Anyway, it was the first thing that came into my head as I stepped off my bike halfway up the aforementioned hill, and was greeted by a man with a pair of binoculars and a hat like a flowerpot. He jumped out of the bushes and began to ask me all sorts of personal questions. He wasn't interested in small talk like, where I was going, where I'd come from and did I know my back axle was buggered? He wanted to know what I did for a living, how much I earned, how many children I had and how many bedrooms there were in my house? In return he told me how he'd been born in Bridgnorth but now lived in Bucks because his wife had left him and run off with the local carpet magnate (two shops, one in Bridgnorth, one in Telford New Town, and a house in Kidderminster with a loft conversion.) And I told him how I was on a cycling trip to escape the traumas of Maynard and Packer where I'd had a torrid affair with the Yugoslav woman who operated the scotch egg machine and had chosen to come on a tour of Shropshire rather than the works' two week self catering package to the holiday village of Nanapoor in Northern Tunisia.

He understood how I felt. He said: 'I always come back here when I'm undergoing an emotional trauma. This place will never change. Bucks has gone under the plough, and the motor car. I've got a mistress in Bracknell now. She's got two kids. One of them's a registered heroin addict.'

At the top of the hill stood a lone corrugated shack. A tree grew out of its middle. From a window patched with a newspaper cutting of Prince Andrew and Sarah Ferguson an old woman's face peered out at me. Smoke was coming from somewhere. It was difficult to tell if she was sitting in front of a log fire or being burned at the stake. The wind made the construction rattle and sway, and there was something unsettling about the whole scene: the dartboard swinging from a lightning tree, the yard cluttered with old fridges, washing machines and ovens ... ovens! damn! I remember now. I didn't turn it off. After I'd taken the baked potato out and then answered the phone to the person who thought I was Timothy Whites, I went back into the kitchen but instead of going to the oven I went to the airing cupboard and turned the immersion heater off, of course, and whilst I was there, I dropped a coathanger down the back of the boiler and as I was fishing around for it I found an old *Daily Mirror* from 1970 and I became so engrossed in the effect decimalisation would have on the small business, and on Arsenal's goal scoring problems, I forgot all about the oven, and when I went back into the kitchen I just grabbed two dessert spoons from the cutlery drawer to use as tyre levers in case of punctures and then ... punctures! Just a minute! I hadn't had a puncture yet. A week's cycling without a puncture? That was unheard of. What was wrong with my tyres? More to the point what was wrong with my back axle? It was still rattling and had developed a wobble. Sometimes I wished I'd bought that tandem and invited a mechanic along for the ride.

I struggled along the top of Wenlock Edge, a cliff-like wedge of rock, the wind fighting me like a hand pushing against my chest, a condition which I was beginning to realise constitutes one of the fundamental laws of cycling i.e. no matter in which direction the cyclist is heading, the wind will always be blowing in his or her face. That is a fact and if you try to get clever and turn round and pedal the other way, the wind will reciprocate.

But cycling also has its pleasures. You can creep up on the wildlife, for instance. Along Wenlock Edge alone I can remember seeing a rabbit, a stoat, a couple of squirrels and numerous field mice and hedgehogs. Unfortunately, they were all flattened, mashed to a pulp by passing Ford Sierras. Hedgehogs of course are the species most frequently involved in this sort of accident, but then it has to be said they do look particularly spectacular when ironed out, rather like those tigerskin hearth rugs: 'Yes, bagged that fella on the B438 just outside Malmesbury. Put up a hell of a struggle, had to pummel him in reverse gear a few times. Tell you what, come and have a look at the Dalmatian I flattened on the B3223 just outside Simonsbath.'

I saw the name Much Wenlock on a signpost and liked it so much I had to go there. I'd planned to have my first night in my Gore-Tex bivibag but I was soaked and took refuge at the first Bed and Breakfast sign I saw. It was a dirty and cheap pub which looked like a railway station and smelt like all pubs seem to do when they're closed, of flat beer and damp walls. On my bedroom door was a sticker – 'This is Jeffs' room' – and under that another, – 'This house is occupied by bores.' The landlord came in and asked me where I was heading and when I told him Lapland, he said: 'You'll be wanting to dry your clothes then,' and he switched on the radiator

An hour later the thing was still stone cold and I lay on the bed shivering and doing my Norwegian study. I was on to sentences now. The translation of:

'Do you have any records by the Brotherhood of Man?' is:

'Har de noen plater av et Brotherhood of Man?'

Lapland isn't renowned for its nightlife. Although, when nights last for four months at a time, the very concept of going out for an evening needs a rethink, and lines like 'make sure you're home by midnight' and 'I think I'll have a night in', take on whole new meanings.

In times gone by Lapps would pass the long evenings in

traditional style, playing games, many of them based around their reindeer culture. Lassooing each other was apparently once very popular.

Times have changed. These days the average reindeer herdsman's idea of entertainment seems to revolve around drinking vast quantities of brandy. 'Biggest bunch of piss-artists north of the Arctic Circle, and I should know,' was how one source described them. The coastal Lapps on the other hand, the ones that live in semis and have Saabs in the garage, are rather more subdued. They prefer to stay in of an evening and watch television. Repeats of British situation comedies dubbed into Norwegian go down very well, 'Are You Being Served', in particular.

In this respect the inhabitants of Much Wenlock have a lot in common with the Coastal Lapps. It was the time of year when people leave their curtains undrawn until late. They sit in their living rooms, eating meals off trays, the electric light shining through the net curtains, and as I walked round the town that evening, the rain making the place look like a limp cardboard box, I saw not one person on the streets, but through every window was the iridescent glow of those familiar 625 lines lodged in the corner of the room and there was Molly Sudgen's blurred but distinctively blue head holding the attention of the inhabitants of Much Wenlock as she no doubt does of those in Hammerfest.

I did meet one man though, who better resembled the nomadic Lapps than the coastal variety. He was leaning against a bar and his name was Clive, Big Clive, Big Big Clive. A taciturn cove who considered talking a waste of good drinking time. You got the feeling he'd like to have been a gentle giant, the problem was he wasn't gentle. He'd sit on something and it would break. He'd pick up a pint pot and the handle would come off in his hand. He'd lean on a cross beam and the whole building would fall down. You know the sort.

The landlord and he, however, were firm friends. The landlord would say something like: 'The trouble with the one-way system in Kidderminster is that it attracts too many cars in from the Stourbridge road rather than sending them round the town to Bewdley. Isn't that right, Clive?'

Clive would grunt and nod, knock an ashtray off the bar and the landlord would move on to discuss traffic flow in Wolverhampton.

It was good beer, well kept. I told the landlord so and he ignored me, but said to Clive: 'You see, Clive, what people don't realise is there's a right and a wrong way of cleaning pipes.' Clive shuffled his feet, searching for a response. He leant nonchalantly against a wall and three horse brasses fell off.

'It's got a good nutty taste,' I said, 'I like nutty beer.'

'You see, the thing is, Clive, the big breweries don't know how to look after their beer, am I right or not?'

Clive had his glass at his lips. The question made him panic. He choked and outside two Ford Sierras collided.

It was a strange triangular conversation between two people only one of whom said anything. I managed to change the subject from beer, to restaurants, to tourism in Shropshire, to local cottage industries, to small breweries and back to beer, and each question I asked, the landlord would direct his answer to Clive and then something would fall over and break.

A boy appeared with a Spanish guitar. He said hello to Clive and his E string snapped. But he fitted another and settled down and played his instrument so beautifully he made me feel hungry. I asked the landlord if he had any bar snacks. Much Wenlock's answer to Segovia was in the corner and I wanted a curry or something.

'You see, Clive, the trouble is that people don't want bar snacks. That's why I converted the backyard into a bistro with real French Cuisine, proper napkins and bread sticks. Isn't that right, Clive?'

Clive coughed and somewhere in the kitchen a pile of plates smashed.

I found another pub that served a warm salad. It was an English summer's evening in the Midlands, folk coming out in overcoats and ski-ing jackets. A man and his wife sat in silence next to me. Then he said: 'Would you rather sit in your usual corner?'

'Aye,' she replied, 'I can chat better over there,' and they shuffled over to their usual corner where they remarked how the summers were once far warmer and sunnier and dryer than they are these days.

But it was marginally warmer and sunnier and dryer the next day as I cycled along the Severn Gorge. I stopped to put my shorts on, a decision the two gentlemen sitting on a bench in Ironbridge would have thought rash:

'Changeable today eh, Michael?'

'Changeable all right,' said Michael, 'I'll tell you how changeable an' all. I sat down on my cap just so as to keep my pants dry and then when I got up to go I left my cap behind. That's how changeable it is!'

I wasn't going to dispute a forecast like that and as soon as the sun disappeared behind a cloud I put my trousers back on.

Ironbridge was the sort of place I didn't really want to visit and yet, as with Stratford-on-Avon, I'd found myself steering inevitably towards it. I think ever since the age of eleven when I returned from the Costa Brava with a suitcase full of bull-fight posters, stuffed donkeys, castanets, sombreros, assorted pennants and leather purses embossed with flamenco dancers, and proceeded to decorate my bedroom in the style of a Lloret de Mar souvenir shop, a room I had to sleep in for the next six years, I've always been irresistibly drawn to tourist attractions. It's annoying really, it means I remember the Castle Cafe and Gift Shop better than the castle itself.

The Ironbridge Gorge, for example, has a revelationary history that with ease transports you back to the beginning of the eighteenth century. In those days timber was industry's most important raw material. But supplies were dwindling and the greatest need was to find a technique for the mass production of iron.

Expense was the problem though; charcoal was the iron industry's main smelting fuel and charcoal was costly. Then in 1709 at Coalbrookdale on the Severn, a brassfounder named Abraham Darby discovered that coal – already mined in the area – could be substituted for charcoal if the impurities were first removed by converting it to coke.

His discovery didn't transform the industry overnight – in fact, Darby kept the secret in his family until 1760 – but slowly founders grew familiar with the process, and under the direction of Darby and people like 'Iron mad' Wilkinson – a man so fanatical about iron he had his own coffin cast in the stuff – the Severn Gorge became the site for twice as many blast furnaces as any other county in the country. Other important industries such as china production at Coalport sprung up, and Darby, having at first been content at the pots-and-pans level of iron founding, decided the world was ready for its first iron bridge. This remarkable project wasn't completed until 1779 and not until Abraham Darby had become Abraham Darby III, but the bridge's opening proved his revolutionary smelting process to the world. It also made life considerably easier for those folk who worked on the north bank of the Severn but lived on the south, and vice versa.

By the end of the Nineteenth Century, though, the gorge was in decline as industry shifted to the conurbations of the Midlands and the North. For years the area crumbled until various trusts moved in with sand and water blasters and pots of paint and begun a restoration programme, from which Ironbridge re-emerged with familiar blue plaques everywhere and the title 'cradle of the industrial revolution'.

And yet, whilst the iron bridge itself looks splendid, and the Museum of Iron and Furnace and the Coalport ovens can only be called grand, restoration on this scale tends to lay a spirit to rest rather than recreate it. As it is, the three giant cooling towers of the Ironbridge Power Station, steaming on the Severn banks further up the gorge and surrounded by hazard lights and Securicor dogs, seem far more of a monument to industry. China production in the gorge is now best represented by mugs with slogans like 'old golfers don't die they just lose their balls'. And industrial innovation has been reduced to machinery such as that found in the public conveniences opposite the iron bridge where you're offered soap, water and hot air all from the same hole in the wall.

I panted my way up and out of the gorge, managing to sidestep Telford, a bowlful of estates, looking very Milton Keynesish to the west. Then the landscape flattened. Ahead, to the north, I could see the chimney stacks and cooling towers that I expected lined the River Trent. The hills of Shropshire were gone. I entered leafy, flat lanes, with good signposts and no traffic except for the occasional twelve-wheeled milk tanker. I was in Staffordshire, and although I'd only been there about five minutes, I could already tell I was going to get on with the place.

1976 was a good year. I remember it well. I was twenty-three and living in Finsbury Park London N5 in a big shared student household. There were three doctors, a dentist, a physiotherapist, a vet and a van driver. I'd like to have been the vet but I was the van driver.

It was a year of motorbikes being dismantled in the living room; of parties full of medical students dressed as nuns and Dracula; it was the year Punk emerged, and it was the year of the intensely hot summer. As a van driver I had one suntanned forearm. I used to be given the overnight run to East Anglia and a girlfriend would come with me and we'd park the van in a field on the Norfolk Broads and spend the night in sleeping bags lying on the piles of printing paper I was carrying. Then, in the morning we'd get going early and stop at a cafe just outside Bungay for a fried breakfast, and it was sunny and hot all day and every day for months.

In the September I boarded a DC10 for New York and hitch-hiked across America to the West coast where I got a job as a salesman for Like Magic Instant Action All Purpose Cleaner For Home, Auto And Industry. It was the most soul-destroying job I ever had and I remember spending Christmas in a motel in Portland, Oregon watching Alistair Sim as Scrooge on television, and then going out to the local Denny's Burger House for Christmas dinner. The only thing that cheered me up was a cassette someone had of one of the best albums of the year, 10cc's 'How Dare You': 'keep me in exile the rest of my days, burn me in hell just as long as it pays. Art for art's sake, money for God's sake. Art for art's sake, money for ... '

'It's two thirty and here are the headlines. Foreign Secretary Geoffrey Howe's peace-keeping mission to South Africa would seem to have failed today after president Botha ... in the opening day of the World Chess Championship between Karpov and Kasparov ... in Telford today firemen had to use ropes to rescue a bullock stuck in a well ... '

It's so annoying the ease with which nostalgia trips you up. There you are cycling through darkest Staffordshire, it's wet and windy and you're heading towards Lapland, and some mealy-mouthed DJ comes on the radio and says: 'We play all the hits', and then churns out an hour of slush from 19-whenever, and without realising it you've climbed aboard the memory train and you're back at that party, on that holiday, in that exam room, in that motel or in that van in the Norfolk Broads and you've stopped pedalling, you're just freewheeling along with a sentimental grin on your face until a tanker covered in dung and the words Liquid Animal Fuel, splashes you with a puddle of mud and snaps you back to the damp reality of 31 July 1986.

I always listened to local radio to find out about the donkey derbys and assorted community events and to hear all the latest gossip, but all the stations were so painfully unoriginal. And if it wasn't nostalgia, it was one of those phone-in shows, a whole programme of lunatics ranting and raving on about how animals should be given the vote and how the world's entire race, hunger and unemployment problems not to mention Aids, would be cured if only people in authority were prepared to drop a few bombs. One of these shows so incensed me I decided I'd phone up and tell them what a skinflint form of radio I thought this was and show them I could be just as abusive as the rest of the callers. I stopped at a phone box. The cord had been cut. At the next one the dial had been jammed. At the third attempt I got through to the radio station but my money wouldn't go in and the line went dead.

On the limits of most towns there's a 'Welcome To' sign, an elaborate affair in many cases, displaying the regional motto and coat of arms and asking the visitor to drive carefully and to look after this town which the residents are proud to live in. Some even announce that they are twinned with European counterparts, a gesture of harmony and detente which makes the traveller feel immediately among friends.

The first sign I saw in Stafford was one written on the side of a bottle bank on the main road into town: 'If you're white that's all right, if you're black fuck off back.'

I'd come into Stafford for medicinal reasons. A few miles previously I'd had a collision with another insect, but this one was a wasp and it flew straight down my t-shirt. One minute I'd been cycling along, proudly in top gear, head up, smug, enjoying the afternoon smells of the farmyards. The next I was wobbling down the road, pounding my chest in Tarzan fashion, my shirt bulging as the prisoner tried to escape. I screeched to a halt ripped my shirt off and the wasp thought about flying off but decided, before it left, it might as well stab me in the belly. I considered putting a puncture repair patch over the wound but instead opted for the ointment on sale in a Stafford chemist.

'I'll have some insect repellent as well,' I said to the assistant. He asked where I was going and when I said Lapland he went:

'Oooh. Lapland!' in a manner that made me want to turn round and go home. 'They've bugs with bites like bear traps in Lapland. However, it is a jolly good place to buy ornamental reindeer hatstands, so I'm told.'

'I'm sleeping out. Do you think I'll need a mosquito net?'

'No point,' he said. 'The smaller mosquitoes can squeeze through the mesh. The bigger ones just lift up the curtain and march under. Only one thing you can tackle them with. Jungle Formula. This large bottle.'

He passed me a pint of the stuff. I said: 'You smear it on liberally I suppose?'

'No, no, what you do is, wait until the mosquito lands on you, then smash it with the bottom of the bottle, like this. Smack! See.'

I bought it and ticked it off the list. I was slowly becoming equipped. Nothing however, could have prepared me for the news that reached me as I sat in a cafe that afternoon. It came over the radio, competing with the juke box, and concerned the effects of radiation cloud that had swept northwards from Chernobyl three months earlier and dumped its deadly load over Northern Scandinavia. The effect was only now being realised and it was a catastrophic blow for the Lapps.

The lichen that their reindeer herds depended on for feed had been seriously contaminated. The reindeer were all but glowing and authorities in Sweden and Norway alone had ordered thirty-eight thousand animals to be slaughtered. Now unsuitable for consumption, they were commercially worthless.

I was straining towards the speakers hanging on the wall, annoyed with everyone for chattering and for the juke box to be playing a song by Madonna during this devastating news. I only caught snippets. It seemed governments were already drawing up proposals to pay the herdsmen compensation, but the problem was more fundamental than that. The effects of the radiation would be present in the soil for years to come. The traditional Lapp lifestyle, based upon the reindeer throughout its history, was under threat. Herdsmen were already reported to be coming into towns looking for work. A traveller to Lapland this summer could well witness the last days of an entire culture.

I was becoming an expert shelterer. Since Stratford-on-Avon it had rained daily and I'd sheltered in some of the prettiest places in The Heart of England. In Ingestre, a country estate just north of Stafford, I was caught in the usual mid-afternoon downpour and pedalled like crazy to a rather grand looking entrance to a livery and stable yard. Two lads were standing under it, repointing the walls.

'Is this your entrance or can anyone shelter under it?' I asked. They said nothing, just carried on working. Then the rain came down in torrents and one said: 'We're going for a cup of tea, coming?'

I followed them through the yard where others were just as busy rebuilding the place. A stables such as these clearly belonged to a manor house, or stately home at one time, but it had fallen into disrepair. I asked who was doing the restoration, and one of the boys said: 'Don't know, we're from Manpower.' He talked while the other one made the tea. He'd done a lot of cycling he said. In fact he'd cycled up here from London: 'I saw this advertisement: "Scientist in Scotland wants cyclist to experiment on," it said. So I thought, sounds like my sort of job, that does; I'll have a go at that, and I set off there and then from Willesden. It was eight o'clock in the evening and by the time I reached here I was shagged out so I stayed. It's the only time I've almost been to Scotland.'

The other lad brought the tea over. He switched on the radio and Chris de Burgh came on singing about his lady in red. 'That's the fourteenth time I've heard that today,' he said and flicked the dial until he found a phone-in show discussing nostalgia. He asked me where I was going.

'Lapland,' I said.

'That's Norway isn't it? I've been to Norway. Hated it. Mind you, the Norwegians hated me, or at least the police did. They threw me out. I got off the boat with no money, no luggage and no shoes and they said I wasn't welcome and told me to go back where I came from. Totally unreasonable if you ask me.'

He'd travelled extensively, he said, and you could tell exactly the sort he was, the sort you meet when you're on foreign soil, miles from anywhere, on some isolated beach or a lonely mountain road. You're really enjoying being away from it all, enjoying being part of this strange new country when suddenly out of nowhere pops this fellow, still with no shoes on and he says: 'Hello, where are you going? Mind if I come with you?' and you're stuck with him for the next fortnight.

India was his favourite place. He'd be out there now he said, but he had to come home every six months to renew his visa. 'Seems totally unreasonable if you ask me. There are Indians who want to stay in this country being sent back to

India; and then there's me, British, who wants to stay in India, being sent back to Britain. Totally unreasonable.'

He liked India, he said, because it was cheap and the weather was better and it was by the sea, which made you wonder if he hadn't missed the point of the place. Now he'd brought out an atlas and was flicking through it page by page recounting his travels: 'Turkey,' he said when he reached a map of Turkey. 'I've been thrown out of there.'

His friend threw his eyes up, mouthed the words 'what a prick,' and rolled a cigarette. We were sitting in what might have once been the groom's quarters. Now they'd been turned into a tea room and the place was a litterbin of PG Tip boxes and digestive biscuit wrappers, but on the wall hung oil paintings of huntsmen and there was a fine marble-topped fire-place.

The lad with the cigarette adopted a Clint Eastwood posture with his feet on the table and said: 'Going to Norway, are you then?' His roll-up fell apart as he spoke. He spat out bits of tobacco.

'I've been thrown out of Norway ... ' interjected his mate.

'Yeah, yeah, we know you've been thrown out of Norway.' He threw his eyes up again and screwed his finger into his head. 'Reckon you'll get there on that bike, do you?'

'Yes,' I said.

He shook his head in the deliberate fashion everyone did when I told them I was going to Lapland and, yes, I was going on that bike.

'Back axles's buggered, you know?' he said. 'Easy job though.'

'Yes, I know. You undo locknut A from cone B, then holding the axle housing still with a wrench at locknut C you screw cone B fully home and then back off one quarter turn, fit in a new axle and reverse the process.'

'Alternatively,' he said, 'you could throw the bike away

and get one like mine.' He spat out a bit of tobacco and left the room.

'I've got a friend in Norway,' said the lad with the atlas. 'His name's Stig. He lives in Bergen. Trouble is I don't know his address. If I had done I probably wouldn't have been thrown out. When you get to Bergen ask for Stig. Tell him you're a friend of Paul's.'

The other one returned. 'This is what you need if you're going to cycle up through Norway,' he said, and he wheeled in a bicycle. But not, dear readers, a bicycle as you and I would know one. The magnificent machine he was now straddled across was a Mountain Bike.

He took it outside and put it thought its paces. 'You could cycle it up stairs if you wanted,' he said, and proceeded to mount a stack of wood, climb over tree stumps and across piles of rubble. The only obstacle that stopped him was the horse he ran into.

He let me have a go. It made my own bike feel like a museum piece. It had fifteen gears, the lowest was like walking on water; the tyres were tough as a tractors'; the brakes sensitive to a twitch.

'How much did it cost?' I asked.

'Five hundred. All the Jamaicans in London have got them.'

'How's that?'

'They nick 'em.'

'I was thrown out of Jamaica.'

'Why don't you shut your bleeding mouth!'

It was good to meet people like this. You could say anything and always get some sort of response, and for that I was grateful. Fortunately, people tended to trust a cyclist on the road. Cyclists were harmless, more so than walkers even. You wouldn't find the Stockwell Strangler out on a cycle ride. As long as I made the initial move locals would be only too keen to waffle on about their village and countryside, despite the fact that more often than not they knew nothing whatsoever about them. People liked the idea of someone touring their area on a bicycle and they wanted to help.

But these were all chance meetings. When I wanted to sit and talk with strangers in the evenings, it was always harder. If you walk into a village pub and sit there and say nothing, the locals tend to react with: 'Who's that suspicious-looking character sitting there saying nothing?' stares. And yet if you sit there and start talking to everyone, they think: 'Who's that suspicious-looking character coming in here and poking his nose in everyone's business?'

Normally in pubs I was of the latter 'sit there and start talking to everyone' fraternity. I don't find it particularly easy, it's not characteristic behaviour, but it's part of the personality I can always recognize emerging when I travel; and when it happens it's always satisfying. Besides, I wasn't finding cycling a particularly gregarious method of travelling and I felt if I didn't grab every conversation I could I'd soon go bonkers.

But that evening in Staffordshire I was feeling self-indulgent. I'd just phoned a girlfriend in Manchester. She'd said I should call in on her, and I really wanted to call in on her. I had some distance to go before then but as I sat in the corner of the Shrewsbury Arms I was already in the warmth and comfort of a flat I'd never been to, surrounded by pot plants and books and a duvet I'd never seen.

In the pub were farmhands and labourers from the local building contractors come straight from work. Their pool balls hit the pockets with a crack and their darts hit the board with a thud, and they passed round snaps of the previous week's tug-of-war competition, in which the Shrewsbury Arms had 'ripped the arms out' of the opposition.

I was surrounded by them but I just sat there and had my sandwiches and read a local magazine: *What's On In*

Uttoxeter. 'Just what is on in Uttoxeter?' I asked the lad standing over me picking his nose with a dart, 'Nothing,' he said, then he dunked one of his Oxo-flavoured crisps into my pickle and walked off.

Bollocks to him. I drank my beer, turned down the barman's offer of a raffle ticket for a joint of beef and said, 'Thanks, goodnight,' and made for the door. As I left I heard a mimicked chorus of 'Thanks, goodnight,' and then someone opened the door after me and blew a raspberry into the night. From now on, I decided, I would buy a raffle ticket whenever I was offered one.

I was staying at a farmhouse. I went into the living room and switched on the light to find the farmer slumped on the couch, asleep. The light woke him. He was only a young man, although already wealthy, having discovered that if you work all night as well as all day you make twice as much money. I'd caught him on his thirty-minute daily break. He asked me what I did for a living and I decided I'd be a scene shifter at the Watford Palace Theatre for the night, which impressed him so much he asked me if I could explain the play on television, it had lost him, he said. I started to watch it. It lost me as well. Within a minute he was asleep. In two minutes so was I.

On the morning when D registration cars first appeared on the road I set out for Derbyshire and the Peak National Park, the day full of overblown cloud, a blue fleck in the sky, and the sun flashing on a Seven-Up can lying in the verge. The forecast was good; this was the change I'd been waiting for; I'd weathered out the wet spell by now, surely. I was growing fit as well; I could feel it. And this was fine country. The hedges looked particularly thick and green that day. Was that a lark singing in that oak? Maybe it wasn't a lark. Maybe it wasn't an oak. Who cares? A man leant on a five bar gate, smoking. A delivery van passed stuffed with provisions from Benfield's the Grocers. Mr Benfield hooted and waved. I waved back. I was really enjoying myself. I started to sing along to In the Summertime by Mungo Jerry on a show playing hits from 1970, then ... creak, wrench, grate, snap, tinkle, bounce.

And finally, disaster.

It's embarrassing to be quite happily cycling along one minute, unhappily cycling along the next, and turning round to see a fractured back axle sticking out of your wheel like a broken bone and ball bearings bouncing down the hill behind you, the next. Embarrassing is the word all right, although ten minutes later when you're still crawling about in the road picking up bits of metal and trying to match their sheared ends together, you realise a more suitable word is, hopeless. I had of course been expecting something like this. Since that crack in the Long Mynd the back axle had been trying to drop the hint that its demise was just around the next corner. And so whilst I wasn't equipped to cope with the problem mechanically, – spare back axles weren't on my essentials list; in fact the only spare anything I had was socks – mentally, I was well prepared. The first thing I did was to go behind the Hawthorn hedge opposite and have a pee; the second was to finish off the Walnut Whip I had my tongue stuck into at the time of the accident, the third part of my master plan involved a decision between 1/ wheeling the bike to the nearest repair shop, and 2/ throwing it in a ditch, abandoning the trip, and spending the summer lying on a beach in Dorset.

I was sitting on the verge trying to feel concerned when, from out of nowhere, onto the scene burst Mr Benfield, the grocer. He took one look at me and said: 'Bike trouble, eh?'

'Yes. But how ... ?'

'Never mind how. We've got to get you to Jim Rowney, and fast.'

Mr Benfield loaded my bike into the back of his van

among the King Edwards and the Dundee cakes and we sped
through the lanes to the village of Rocester, where I was
dropped outside a blue door.

'Jim Rowney will look after you,' said Mr Benfield. 'Jim
Rowney's been fixing bikes since he was this high.'

I knocked on the door. An old woman appeared, then an
old man – if he was Jim Rowney he was still this high. They
huddled next to each other in the doorway.

'Is Jim Rowney in?'

'Who?'

'Jim Rowney.'

'Who?'

'Jim Rowney.'

'Who?'

Jim Rowney.'

'Who?'

'I want my bike fixed.'

'What?'

'I want my bike fixed.'

'Something wrong with your bike?'

'Yes.'

'Jim Rowney's the man for that.'

'Is he in?'

'Is who in?'

Sigh.

Eventually I got through on the phone to a cycle shop in
Ashbourne. They'd send someone out they said. But not for
an hour or so.

'So what do you suggest I do for an hour or so in
Rocester?' I asked the trio of teenage girls sitting on the wall
outside the chip shop. 'This is my first visit and I want to do
something memorable.'

'You could sit here all day like we do,' said the
spokeswoman; she thought about it some more: 'Can't think
of anything else.'

But she underestimated her village. There's lots to do in Rocester. To begin with you can visit the Queen's Arms and the Red Lion. Alternatively you can visit the Red Lion and then the Queen's Arms. In fact you could easily fill up your hour and a half commuting between the two. But instead, why not have a salad sandwich at Benfield's the grocers? The counter staff are all really pleasant and they all wear green overalls similar in design to Mr Benfield's. Clutching your sandwich you can then cross the road and walk down to the recreation ground where the three old men sitting on the bench will engage you in conversation. Unfortunately they speak some strange Staffordshire dialect that probably only Vikings understand and so you don't come away spiritually enriched or anything, but it does waste about ten minutes. I tried out some Norwegian on them, from the 'Making Friends' section of the phrase book:

'*Hvilke forretninger driver De med?*'
('What kind of business are you in?')
And I'm sure they replied:
'*Har De barnemeny?*'
('Do you have a children's menu?')

At the other end of the recreation ground sitting on a concrete base you'll find the rather unlikely resting place for the Kowloon-Canton Railway Steam Engine No. 67., The Hong Kong Flyer, its engine long ago cannabalised, graffiti smeared over its boiler and its lagging showing. And then, above it in a nearby field is a rather more modern monument to the machine age, a bizarre sculpture commissioned by JCB Ltd., the plant manufacturers whose giant factory overshadows Rocester from the other side of the River Dove. The sculpture has the design of a lunar landing module, a mechanical insect with shovels for legs. A local's review of it as a work of art was given me by one of Mr. Benfield's assistants: 'It cost £80,000 and it's horrible.'

Then if you've any time to spare there's the local

archeological museum which displays the finds of Rocester's Roman dig. Originally the village was a Roman fort built to defend the Peak District metal mines. Now the remains are housed in a disused chapel where a ferret-like fellow sits sloughing the muddy and ancient residue from fragments of pottery which he then pieces together like a fifteen-hundred year-old jigsaw, and concludes that the Romans ate out of bowls and drank from beakers.

When you've done that and been back for another salad sandwich at Mr Benfield's you'll find your time will be up. I rejoined the three girls still sitting on the chip shop wall.

'It's a nice place, Rocester,' I said. 'I think I'll come here for my honeymoon.' But as the van from the cycle shop drew up and my bike and I were loaded up and driven off towards Ashbourne, I knew I'd never come back to Rocester again in my life. You can tell with some places.

'Well I'll go to Fleetwood on a tram,' said Henry, the little man's favourite expression and delivered in a treacle-thick Derbyshire accent that had been a shock when I'd first heard it. The accent in Rocester had been nowhere nearly so broad and I had the feeling I'd crossed far more than a county border on the drive in the van. On a bicycle you have the time to taste the countryside. In a car you swallow it whole.

'Well, I'll go to Fleetwood on a tram,' repeated Henry. My bicycle was lying on its back with its wheels in the air on the operating table at the rear of Kennedy's cycle shop. Henry was squinting at the guts that lay in neat piles all around him, his whole face screwed up in consternation. 'Your block's buggered as well as your back axle; you'll need a new one ... unless ... I suppose it's worth a try,' and he was off again, burrowing eagerly into the back wheel.

Henry was about four foot eleven and looked like Arthur Lowe. He'd started working for Kennedy's forty years ago in the days when: 'We had bikes lined up out there waiting to

be repaired. I used to work on nothing but bikes then, I did.'
No wonder his eyes had lit up when I wheeled my stricken
velocipede into his work shop. Kennedy's was a glorified
hardware store now, and I'd found Henry surrounded by
aluminium buckets and mole traps, concentrating his efforts
on relocating a broom handle into its brush.

'I spend most of my day filling Calor Gaz stoves now. I
hardly get any bikes in any more, nobody seems to … well,
I'll go to Fleetwood on a tram.' The block became unstuck
and drove the wheel round once more.

'Tricky job that was,' he said, packing in some new ball
bearings and slipping in an appropriately sized new back
axle. 'See, most people would have undone the locknut A
from cone B, then, holding the axle housing still with a
wrench at locknut C, screwed cone B fully home and then
backed it off a quarter turn. Not me though. I'm a "loosen
locknut B, then screw cone C and back off locknut A one
quarter" man, myself.' Then he stood back and squinted at
the bike again and said: 'Well, I'll go to Fleetwood on a tram.
I don't like the look of that chain,' and off he burrowed once
more.

Henry used to be a member of the Ashbourne cycle club:
'We used to cycle to Liverpool and back in a day. 'Course
there was a fraction of the traffic then.' His bike in those days
was a fixed chain, not a gadget on it. I told him about the
Mountain Bike and his eyes lit up: 'Ooer, I'd love a Mountain
Bike. I could get round my new garden a treat.'

He fixed the chain and turned his attention to the spokes.
'I've just moved house, you see. I'm a bachelor and moving
is one hell of a palaver, but I've got this grand garden. Here,
come and have a look.' And he led me up the alley to a fence,
and through a hole pointed to an extensive new housing
estate in the distance. 'See those houses?'

'Yes.'

'The one in the middle's mine.'

'Oi! we haven't got all bloody day you know.' The boss's voice made us both jump. Henry scurried back into his work shop: 'Just my luck that is. I spend all day in here and the one time I poke my nose through the fence to look at my new house he catches me. I'll go to Fleetwood on a tram.'

Henry spent about two hours on my bike. Apart from replacing the back axle, he tightened the chain, put a new tyre on, replaced a handful of broken spokes and oiled and generally serviced it. Afterwards there were three nuts and a washer left over.

'What shall I do with these?' I said.

'Throw them in the bin, of course,' said Henry.

The cost was ten pounds inclusive of the van to come and pick me up.

'I can't believe it's so little,' I said to the manager when he presented me with the bill. 'Henry's spent so much time on it. He's done so much.'

'That's Henry for you.'

'He certainly knows his stuff.'

'He takes too bloody long.'

Henry saw me off on the high street. 'Where you going any road?' he said.

'Lapland.'

He nodded. 'I should get myself a bell if I were you then.'

Where does the North of England begin? How does one define the ingrained difference between the North and the South? From reading *North Country*, a book I'd found in a War on Want shop, a book that smelt wonderfully of lofts and old *Hotspur* annuals, the author Edmund Vale would appear to have spent a long time sitting in a chair, smoking a pipe and contemplating such questions:

'It is hard to say why the North should be any more romantic than the South, East or West. Perhaps it is our Viking bias that we can never get rid of. Perhaps it is a respect for those qualities that are essentially Northern: grit, steeliness, enthusiasm fostered under conditions of hard living and hard weather.'

The line which marks the start of the North, he draws on the southern bounds of Yorkshire and Lancashire, roughly stretching between the Mersey and the Humber, a demarcation he reaches by process of elimination: 'Lincolnshire? Eastern counties. Nottingham? Midlands. Derbyshire? Doubtful. Derbyshire is the most difficult to place. The Pennines, which are the strength of the North Country, originate here, and the people have a great deal in common with their neighbours of Lancashire and Yorkshire. But the spirit of Derbyshire is something that has never quite been committed to the Midlands or the North.'

The book was published in 1937 but Mr Vale's observations are still germane. Derbyshire is an island of a county. That boundary I felt myself cross the previous day may not have been the start of the North but it was certainly the end of everything else. I was no longer cycling through a lush, tree-filled belly of nature; the countryside didn't feel fat any more. There was an underlying greyness about it now, in the stone walls, the villages and the moorland. The land was stretched tightly, a thin skin covering the rock. And the most dramatic change of all was the peaked horizon: I was cycling towards mountains now.

I say cycling. In fact, I was hardly moving. The sun was out but the clouds were being flung across the blue by an icy wind that was growing ever stronger. It was the second day of August and yet most of the cottages in the Peak villages had smoke rising from their chimneys, and the wind blew the trails horizontal; in a number of cases it had blown the chimneys horizontal as well. Ice cream signs were thrown across garage forecourts. Somewhere in Staffordshire a fisherman was killed by a falling tree. Trying to climb a hill was like cycling through sand and then going down the other side was just as arduous. I pushed my bike for a few miles but then hid in a cafe.

A couple parked their Ford Sierra outside then came in and manoeuvred themselves onto the table next to mine. They had overcoats on.

'How do,' said the man, then snatched the menu off his wife, 'I think I'll have the pork.'

'Don't have the pork. We're going to have pork at home tonight.'

'I'd rather have that pork tomorrow for breakfast. It's Sunday.'

'We've got kidney for breakfast. Perhaps we could have some pork now and then have the other cold tomorrow.'

'Our Hilda doesn't like cold. It's a fad. On second thoughts I'll have eggs.'

'You had eggs for breakfast. Save the eggs then we can have the pork for lunch at home and have the kidneys in a steak and kidney when we get back tonight.'

'Why don't we have the goulash now and then have the pork in sandwiches for supper and a kedgeree for breakfast?'

'Because, if you have kedgeree you'll cause a fuss, have the sausages now and we'll have the pork in a goulash on Monday.'

'What about them herb sausages we bought up from Eastbourne?'

'You can have them for breakfast with ... '

Hang on! Hang on! Did he say Eastbourne?

Yes, they came from Eastbourne. They'd moved down from these parts for work, but he'd been laid off and they'd retired early. They were back visiting relatives. 'The only reason people move down South,' she said, 'is for work or for marriage.' She spoke of their existence down there as if they were in exile.

But I could understand what she meant. I was already beginning to notice I'd taken on a fascination value. People were suddenly treating me like a foreigner and taking it upon themselves to give me a good impression. I wasn't sure if this was a difference between the North and the South of England, or simply the experience of a stranger in a strange land. Whatever it was, I was grateful for the welcome.

Never more so than in Brassington, the village I wheeled my bike into that afternoon. It was the last day of the Brassington Wakes, and the gala day had become a battle between the garden fête in one corner and the force seven gale in the other. Stalls were being blown over, flags were wrapped in knots round lamp-posts, dresses and ties were up around necks, a balloon was ripped out of a child's hand and was up and over the moors in seconds.

But it was a colourful and local celebration of a pretty village. Everyone seemed to be carrying potted plants and cakes around with them and I immediately wanted to stay, so I found a Bed and Breakfast and joined in.

A man came over and offered me raffle tickets: 'For the church roof,' he said. I wasn't sure if I was contributing towards its repair or going to win the thing outright, but I bought a strip and he said, ' Good luck, I hear it's a strong field today.'

Strange thing to say, I thought, although the woman on the 'guess the weight of the fire engine' stall had said something similar, 'Good luck in the race,' I think. Then I noticed that the kids were looking at me in awe and everyone was nodding in a friendly fashion and saying things like: 'He must be fit,' and then when I heard over the loud speakers that the fell race was about to begin and that contestants should assemble at the St John's ambulance tent I realised my tracksuit bottoms and trainers had labelled me a fell runner. In desperation I ducked inside the tea tent.

'Piece of strawberry flan please.'

'You'll have to eat it quick,' said the helper, 'They're starting in a minute.'

Outside I peered through the crowd and saw skinny runners peeling off track suits. A man with an Official's badge said to me: 'You know the route don't you? It's well marked anyway.' And I tried to say, 'I'm not a fell runner! I used to cheat at school cross countries. I couldn't run up one of those hills, it would kill me,' but with a mouthful of strawberry flan all I got out was 'mnnmnnnnnm'. I heard the starter shout: 'On your marks ... ' and in a moment of panic I went to the Gents.

There was a queue. 'Want to buy a raffle ticket?' said the lad in front of me.

'I've already got five.' I showed them to him.

'They're for the church roof.'

'What are yours for?'

'Climbing frame for the play school.'

I bought a strip off him and then he turned and gave the toilet door an almighty thump.

'C'mon Greg, we're pulling in five minutes. ... you win a bottle of sherry, by the way. Sandeman, I think, or Cockburns or something, don't drink the stuff myself ... C'mon Greg, for god's sake ... you pulling this afternoon?'

'Pulling what?'

'Tug-o-war.'

'No ... no ... I'm not a fell runner either.'

'Thought I'd seen you pulling for the Miner's. Bunch of women the Miner's are.'

'Who do you pull for?'

'The Knockerdowns ... c'mon Greg what are you doing, you've not fallen asleep again have you? ... ' The cistern flushed. Greg came out doing up his trousers. As soon as he saw me he said: 'Want to buy a raffle ticket?'

The fell race was eventually won by a fourteen-year-old Alf Tupper. I joined the crowd leaning over him as he was revived by the St John's Ambulance. The woman whose Bed and Breakfast I'd booked into turned up and said to me: 'I hear you did very well.' She introduced me to her friends and they all said: 'Well done. I hear it was a very close run thing.'

But attention was quickly switched to the tug-o-war field where the teams were lining up. The Miner's Arms appeared. They weren't exactly a bunch of women, in fact they were a bunch of big, fat, unshaven, smelly, hairy men who belched a lot and wore steel capped boots, but compared to the Knockerdowns there was I suppose something vaguely effeminate about them, a certain sensitivity.

The Knockerdowns were all square blocks. Not one of them had a neck. They were all ninety percent shoulders, ten percent thighs. One of them had a Slimcea Calorie-controlled Crispbread t-shirt stretched across him.

The anchor men took the strain. Each team had about eight pullers and one by one they dug their heels in and took up the tension on the rope until the veins stood out on their necks. The referee raised his hanky. His underarms were swamps of sweat. The crowd hushed. A Miner sneezed. A Knockerdown grated his teeth. The ref. dropped his arm and there was a loud grunt, followed by a loud groan followed by the entire Miner's Arms team falling over.

But it was the Miner's Arms I found myself in later. It was Saturday night and I had my best on, although any attempt to impress sartorially was bound to suffer from the sharp smell of insect repellent that now wafted from all my clothing, the result of an improperly secured top to my bottle of Jungle Formula. Mind you there were no flies within miles of me.

I asked for a pint and the landlady said: 'Good race this afternoon?' and then she sniffed the air around me and gave me an odd look. But I was already in her good books. I'd just ordered a plate of her homemade Saturday Night Special, red cabbage and potato hash. I'd seen the portion put in front of the man eating at the table in the corner, a man I recognised from the Miner's tug-o-war team. It wasn't so much a plate as a trough, and I was in the mood for a trough.

'I'll have whatever he's having,' I'd said, and sat down next to him. He was the anchor man, I remembered, and an anchor was a good way to describe him. His shoulders hung stiff at his side, too musclebound to swing. He sat there ladling his hash to his face with one arm, the other wrapped protectively around the remaining lake in front of him. Bits of cabbage clung to his cardigan and each mouthful he took he made a noise like the tide going out.

'How do?' I said.

He looked at me and nodded. 'Weren't you in the fell race this afternoon?'

But when my meal arrived it was in a bowl of a civilised size. I had a soup spoon and bits of bread with the crusts cut off. And my red cabbage was in a little cocktail glass.

'I thought I was going to get one like you,' I said.

'You've got to be a big man to get one like this. If you don't want all that bread by the way, I'll have it to wipe up with.'

Cynth, his wife, joined him, then his daughter and son-in-law and some friends of theirs from Filey. Then a niece whose husband wouldn't make it tonight she said because he'd yet to regain consciousness from the lunchtime session.

'Aren't you the lad who won the fell race this afternoon?' said Cynth.

'No, I'm on a bicycle. Just passing through Brassington.'

'*Brassington*,' announced a man next to me in a three piece suit not a piece of which matched, '*Brassington*,' with a short A.'

'*Brassington*,' I said, pinching the first syllable.

'Interesting place, Brassington ... ' he went on.

'No it isn't ... ' said a voice behind him.

' ... No-one's quite sure where the name comes from. The locals of course call it Brasson – Brason being the old Peak word for Man with one leg. Although as far as I can recall no one-legged person has ever been connected with the history of the village.'

'That's a horrible pullover,' said the anchor man's niece, prodding me in the ribs. 'Smells of mothballs or something. Do you want to buy a raffle ticket by the way? It's for the W.I. minibus.' I bought a strip. The pub grew busier. Our table for four had twelve round it. It was the last night of the Brassington Wakes and this lot, who seemed to have been drinking all day, were now going to continue into the night, and they were insistent that I should swim alongside them. A lad called Pete sat down next to me and said: 'Aren't you him what won the fell race?'

'No, no, I'm on a bicycle. First time in Brassington.'

'That's better. *Brassington.*' said the man in the suit. 'But try rolling the tongue around that short A. *Brassington.*'

'*Brassington.*'

'Of course many people think that Brassington came from the term Brassy, meaning very cold, because we get some bad winters round here you know, but in fact the term Brassy comes from the old naval expression to Freeze the Balls of the Brass Monkey, which has nothing whatsoever to do with testicles but concerns the brackets used to house cannonballs at sea and which, if allowed to freeze, contract and dislodge their balls, therefore all theories connecting the term to the derivation of Brassington can be discounted.'

'You reckon those are tights or stockings?' said Pete, eyeing a girl with fishnet all over her legs. She saw me looking at her and she said: 'Do you know I've got a doberman who eats twenty pounds of meat a week?'

'I reckon they're tights,' I said.

'I've an idea they're stockings,' said Pete.

The girl was leaning over the table now talking to Cynth: 'here! no more to drink for you, you'll be falling off your roof again.'

'Smile,' said Cynth and she took a snap of me with her Instamatic, then toppled into her son-in-law. 'This is Mick. Mick this is Mark. He won the fell race today on a bicycle.'

'Good pub, this,' said Mick, draining his pint. 'That's number ten I think. Got to be careful, 'cos I'm driving, see.'

'Of course the interesting thing about this pub, the Miner's Arms,' continued the man in the three piece, 'is that the miner's lamp depicted on the sign outside would suggest that it's a coal miner's pub, whereas the only mining in this area is for lead, and has been since Roman times.'

'I'm sure those are stockings,' said Pete.

The anchor man prodded me and said: 'I've got a Mercedes Benz and I can't read nor write.'

'No and you can't bloody drive either,' said his wife.

The girl with the fishnet legs was now sitting on the lap of her husband's best friend and nibbling his ear: 'My doberman once ate three pounds of rump steak and then went straight out and bit the head off a Pekinese,' she said to him. He ran his hand up her leg and grinned when he reached a suspender.

'See, I knew they were stockings,' said Paul. Then he leaned over me and said: 'Can I ask you a personal question? What's that aftershave you're wearing?'

'Er ... Jungle Formula,' I said. 'Jungle Formula, For Men.'

'Everyone wearing that down South, are they?'

'Yes. Bit racey for Brassington, is it?'

'Almost right,' said the man in the three piece. 'Just roll the tongue and have a harder contact on the B: *Brassington.*'

'*Brassington.*'

'Better.'

'Many people of course include Brassington in the Peaks, whereas the Peaks aren't an area at all. The Peaks were a tribe that lived ... '

I had a lot of beer and fell for the barmaid. I chatted to her as she washed up and suddenly discovered I was the last person in the pub. I suggested I walk her home. It was a clear and cold moonlit night.

'Aren't you the one who won the fell race this afternoon?' she said.

'Yep, that's me.'

I saw her to her door. She lived directly opposite my Bed and Breakfast.

'Where are you cycling to?' she said.

'Lapland.'

'Why?'

'Er ... for charity. Local church roof fund.'

'What's the best place you've been to so far?'

'Brassington,' I said, and effortlessly slipped in the short A. I thought about kissing her goodnight but she said:

'Are you wearing fly spray?'

'Yes.'

'Thought so.' And she was quickly into her house. I could see her in her bedroom from my own across the street. She came to the window and drew the curtains and a few minutes later the light went off.

And Brassington was the best place I'd come across so far. I'd been in that wonderful position of Just Passing Through. People hadn't asked me much but had told me everything. I thought about staying another day but for someone who'd said he was heading for Lapland I thought I might be pushing my luck to be still in the Miner's Arms the following lunchtime. Besides, I had the feeling no-one would be able to remember who I was.

So next morning I got moving again early. The barmaid's curtains were still drawn as I wheeled my bike out of the village. At the top of the hill I looked back once then climbed on the bike and put pressure on the pedals. As I did so the back wheel slipped out and bits of back axle dribbled onto the tarmac. 'Well I'll go to Fleetwood on a tram,' I said, and cursing the little man from Ashbourne who looked like

Arthur Lowe and had once cycled to Liverpool and back in a day, I undid locknut A from cone B, held the axlehousing still at locknut C, then screwed cone B fully home and backed it off one quarter turn, all by myself, and it worked just fine.

4. The Pennines: Brakes

I was back on course again, climbing steeply and heading north through the beautiful Monsal Dale where every telephone box had been freshly painted. A real treat for any vandals on holiday.

Lapland was getting steadily nearer and my Norwegian steadily more fluent. I was now confident At The Tobacconist's and At The Filling Station and could get by At the Business Luncheon.

And my knowledge of traditional Lapp customs was becoming ever more comprehensive. I knew that the manufacture and adornment of reindeer horn implements is the most characteristic Lapp art form. I was well aware that the parents of a Skolt Lapp bride would give a dowry of a fishing net or a sledge. And it was common knowledge as far as I was concerned that in the not too distant past the Lapps had practiced euthanasia, ('the blessed journey' they called it, the ceremonial pushing of the elderly over a precipice or through a hole in the ice). Now, on a Sunday afternoon near Bakewell, I was sitting on a stone wall eating a bag of fruit and familiarising myself with Lapp religious customs.

The old Lapp religion was the animism typical of Arctic races. All things had a soul and power over men's lives, and the most fearsome gods were the great forces of nature: the sun, thunder, wind, fertility and sickness. The Lapps worshipped at a sacrificial site where an idol was enclosed by a semi-circle of antlers, and an altar was erected and smeared with fish heads, blood and entrails.

Religious practice in Derbyshire is nothing like that. Fish heads and entrails don't come into it. Although a unique sort of folklore does, the ancient art of well-dressing.

I saw the advert in a local paper, the *Derbyshire Telegraph*, on the same page as the results of a survey which gave conclusive evidence that more homes in the East Midlands owned a washing machine than in any other part of the country. 'Bradwell Well-dressing. Sunday 6 p.m.' the announcement read. Bradwell? I'd seen the name some-where. I looked up. In the distance, to the North, were the beginnings of the Pennines, the colossus of Kinder Scout, its top hidden by cloud. Much nearer, just across the road in fact, was a signpost: Bradwell, 2 miles.

A number of villages in Derbyshire still dress their wells, a tradition that originated in medieval times. These villages are all on limestone and rain soaks quickly through into the earth. Reliable wells were once vital and each community held an annual thanksgiving ceremony for water.

To begin with, flowers were simply thrown into the well. Then it became popular to create elaborate dressings. The blessing of Bradwell's wells goes back to 1701, and now incorporates a gala of festivities. All the previous week there had been dances, barbecues, ferret races, cricket matches, coffee mornings, and bring-and-buy sales, and tonight was the well-dressing itself, the spiritual highlight.

Bradwell has three wells and each had been dressed depicting a Biblical scene. 'In Litton they just do a cathedral, but that's easy,' said the woman knitting a pullover in the church market. 'In Bradwell our wells tell whole stories.'

The procession started at the Church Street well which was dressed with a vivid interpretation of the Song of Simeon. Laid on a clay base the pictures were made up from alder cones, corn kernels, seeds and leaves and barks of all sorts, and then coloured with thousands of petals. And they were so beautifully fresh, they could only just have been completed.

'If they're put out too early the weather always gets to them. The clay starts to crack,' said the woman letting me share her brolly. 'That's what happened last year. You know I'm sure the summers were dryer and warmer when I was a ... '

I lost her as the Castleton Brass Band struck up with an almighty thump on the bass drum and the procession began its march through the village, a line of girl guides and clergymen, of blue anoraks and multi-coloured golf umbrellas.

With the methodist minister and the vicar taking it in turns to conduct proceedings we passed the Townend well, where the beheading of John the Baptist was shown in glorious technicolor. Then up to the Swaledale dressing, a depiction of Solomon annointing Saul, where we sang a verse of two of 'The Day Thou Gavest Lord Hath Ended' with a solo from a waterlogged tuba, and then after a moment's respectful hesitation we all filed into the pub opposite where I spent the evening discussing rather more secular matters i.e. cement and its role in the Twentieth Century.

The Blue Circle Cement works is a big, ugly industrial eyesore that dominates Bradwell physically and spiritually. A large percentage of the village works there, and at night it's lit up like some shrine. Blue Circle had even sponsored the carnival queen. Their name was emblazoned across her sash.

'Cement is just ground limestone and shale that's been burnt ... ' said the man who looked like Fred Flintstone, leaning in an erudite pose against the pub fireplace. We'd just completed a tour of the lounge bar's walls during which he'd meticulously identified the different grades of cement and knocked over Mrs Brathay's Mackeson. ' ... and yet it's played a major role in the shape of the world. Empire State

Building: Cement. Sidney Opera House: Cement. Eiffel Tower: Cement.'

'Metal.'

'What?!'

'The Eiffel Tower. I think you'll find it's metal.'

'Metal?'

'Yes.'

'What, all of it?'

'Yes. All of it.'

'Are you sure?'

'Sure.'

'I always thought it was cement.'

'No. Definitely metal.'

'Typical bloody Frogs.'

Blue Circle Cement featured heavily the next morning as well, as I struggled up Snake Pass and lorry loads of the stuff blundered past me, dripping and groaning. I imagined myself flattened like a hedgehog or knocked into the ditch amongst the graveyard of sheep already lying there with Leyland radiator grills imprinted on their foreheads. In fact Snake Pass must have witnessed more than its fair share of carnage as nature met hot metal head on, but now after almost two weeks on the road, I was growing accustomed to it all; it had reached the stage where I could only identify animals if they were squashed into two dimensions.

The road followed the perimeter of Lady Bower reservoir, Manchester's water supply, and then began to climb steadily, although the gradient was hardly back-breaking. In Bradwell, everyone had said: 'Snake Pass on a bicycle? You must be mad!' and as I rounded each corner I kept expecting to see the black tarmac ribbon ahead of me suddenly take off into the sky. But it never did. I cycled steadily up to the chilly and desolate peat bogs of the 1680-foot summit with no trouble at all, and set off almost immediately on the descent.

Ahead of me was Manchester and the nurse I'd met windsurfing in Greece six weeks previously.

You know what holiday romances are. You meet someone on a two week package to the Aegean. You're wearing your new Hawaian shirt and she's got sun bleached hair and is as brown as a bar of Bourneville, and you spend the evenings doing ridiculous ethnic dances and smashing crockery, and you drink a few pints of retsina each and show each other your white bits. And you think what a wonderful, carefree, exciting, vivacious and beautiful person. We must keep in touch. And when you get back to England you phone each other up and arrange to meet one miserable October evening in La Plaka restaurant on Tottenham Court Road where there's a picture of Athens in rush hour on the wall and the only music they have is Nana Mouskouri's Greatest Hits. And you're waiting there with your suntan long gone, your lithe, beachboy's body blotchy and podgy under pullovers and overcoats, bags under your eyes, your Access statement came that morning and the most exciting thing to have happened to you since your holiday was seeing Dickie Davies in a lift. Then into the bar walks this vision, all eyes are on her as she walks across the room and sits at an empty table clearly waiting for someone special. You can't believe it's her, and of course it isn't. There behind her, standing in the doorway, is your Rachel, the one with the snivels and the kleenex stuffed up her sleeve, thermal tights and not a trace of blonde left. She tells you about her new job in Sketchley's. You tell her about Dickie Davies. She shows you her holiday snaps and you show her yours and you both tacitly decide you're never going to go away with Intasun again.

But I was going to risk a reunion, and now I was freewheeling down Snake Pass at speed. This was partly due to enthusiasm, but mostly due to brake failure.

*

'Come in,' said Nurse Grimes, 'would you like to go to the toilet or anything?'

'No thanks.'

'How about a cup of herb tea, made with soft water, not the hard stuff you get down south?'

'No thanks.'

I sat down on the couch in a manner that I hoped would convey I wanted to stay at least three days. She looked lovely and it was so good to see her. 'So this is Manchester!?' I said.

'How about a bowl of All-bran then? I was just going to have one myself.'

'No thanks.'

She sat down on the couch and said: 'I don't like that pullover.' Then she looked at me the way only a nurse can: 'How long are you going to stay?'

'Well, I've got to fix my brakes. Might take a day or two, or three, I'm a lousy mechanic, see?'

'Are you really going to Lapland?'

'Yes, but I'm in no hurry.'

'You won't eat the lichen will you?'

The news from Lapland wasn't good. A land that few people could have pointed out on the map the week before was suddenly high profile in all the media, but for all the wrong reasons. All week there'd been pictures in the press and on television of scientists crouching over slaughtered reindeer testing the degrees of radioactivity. Some animals were carrying up to 15,000 bequerels of caesium 137 per kilo, when the permitted maximum is thirty. The Lapp herdsmen were beginning to realise the dreadful truth and, after the initial shock, were growing angry.

'Make sure you eat lots of high fibre and you should be all right,' said Nurse Grimes. 'Here, have a Newberry Fruit.' She held a box under my nose, 'they're from Mrs Hardcastle. She's just had her gallstones taken out. Your hair's grown

since you were in Greece. Do you think we're going to get
on?'

'Yes.'

'If we don't we should admit it.'

'Right.'

'And one of us should leave.'

'Right ... we'll toss for it.'

She had a studio flat. She allocated me a cardboard box in
a corner of the kitchen to put my stuff in. It was marvellous.
I felt like a dog with his own basket. I unpacked and
immediately the flat was a tip. I said: 'I think you should
know now I'm prone to untidiness,' and then I emptied my
panniers into the washing machine.

'I think you'll enjoy Manchester,' she said. 'We can go and
see the ship canal. And there's a good Marks and Spencers in
the city centre you might like to have a look at.' Then she put
on her uniform and went to work. 'Make yourself at home,'
she said.'

I started off in the kitchen, making myself at home there.
Then I made myself at home in the sitting room-cum-
bedroom. Then I made myself at home in the bathroom with
shower fitting. Then, having made myself at home in the
area by the stereo-cassette player, I went back into the
kitchen and made myself at home there all over again.

Manchester. The third city in England. Born of the industrial
revolution, it was the workshop of the nation during the
cotton boom of the Nineteenth Century, a city of chimneys
belching out industrial waste for more than a hundred years.
Then cotton declined, the city went smokeless and as the air
cleared the Arndale Centre rose from the ashes.

It stood rooted like a monolith, straddled across the city.
Stacks of shops, fifteen acres of concrete and coloured glass,
a natural landmark. Ask anyone for directions in Manchester
and they'll begin: 'Well, you know the Arndale?'

'Will Jeremy Watson please go to the information centre. His mother is getting tired of waiting for him,' said the loud-speaker. Most of the time the Arndale had this feel of a fairground or a circus. All street life was here and in the precincts adjacent. There were mimes, buskers and preachers, and, in the middle of one piazza, a young kid in tramp's clothes drawing cartoons on the pavement. I pointed to one character he'd drawn and asked who it was supposed to be.

'Donald Duck,' he said.

'Donald Duck?!'

'Aye, Donald Duck.'

'It doesn't look anything like Donald Duck.'

'It does an' all. There's the beak, there's the tail and there are his feet.'

'No, sorry.'

His face crumpled. 'I'm only nine.'

'Pardon.'

'I'm only nine. What do you expect, a masterpiece?'

I gave him twenty pence and continued my tour of Manchester cycle shops. I'd had a look at my brakes that morning, taken off the parts I'd thought were faulty and gone in search of replacements. But these were old brakes:

'I'm looking for some spare parts like these,' I said in the first shop, proffering a handful of embarrassingly worn bits.

'We don't keep them anymore,' said the assistant.

'Any idea where I might get some?'

'You could try Sotherby's.'

I looked everywhere and ended up in the suburbs, in the Old Trafford district. As I passed the cricket ground, home of Lancashire CC., I noticed the roses match, Lancashire versus Yorkshire, was in play and I sat in on the afternoon session. The turnout was poor considering the derby nature of the game, but the support that there was, was deeply rooted. These were county men and there was nothing they liked to do more than beat each other at cricket.

The sun was out intermittently but there was a chilling wind. 'A pleasant autumnal day' the weatherman had said.

'Quite a pleasant autumnal day, is this,' said the man next to me. He was sitting there with his shirt off, displaying a tattoo that said, 'Jim'. He'd come to see every match this summer and his neck and forearms had been weatherbeaten into a tan, but this just highlighted how ghostly pale the rest of his torso was. 'Cricket's not what it used to be,' he said.

'Bugger Yorkshire,' shouted a ten-year-old supporter a few rows down.

'Watch your language,' shouted Jim. 'Supporters aren't what they used to be neither. Bloody weather's gone downhill an' all,' He put his shirt back on. 'Lost a lot of play through rain this season, we have. It's the adiabatic lapse rate what does it, you know.'

'The what?'

'Adiabatic lapse rate. Rain clouds steam in from the Irish sea and then dump their load as they rise to climb the Pennines. Manchester gets it bad, but you should live in Rochdale if you want to see rain.'

The Yorkshire wicket keeper, Bairstow, held a good catch. 'Fuck off Bairstow,' shouted the ten-year-old below us.

'Watch your language,' shouted Jim. 'If my kid spoke like that I'd grate his blanes,' – or something like that.

'You're one of them Southerners, aren't you?' he said.

'Yes.'

'This is Manchester, this is.'

'Yes.'

'Well?'

He wanted my opinion and so I said: 'It's a big city. It's got shopping precincts, multi-storey car parks, ring roads, a Sainsburys ... '

'And a Waitrose.'

' ... and a Waitrose.'

'And a Safeway's.'

'And a Safeway's.'

'A couple of Fine Fare's.'

'A couple of Fine Fare's.'

'Not to mention the Tesco's in Didsbury.'

'It's also got housing estates, and waste ground and lots of traffic.'

He thought about this and nodded. 'Used to be a Presto's once as well.'

'I like Mancunians though,' I said. 'In fact I like Northerners in general. They seem to have a lot of time for you.'

'That's 'cos most of 'em are without work.'

Yorkshire were batting out for a draw. Jim was getting bored: 'What're you doing here, any road?'

'Got to get the brakes fixed on my bicycle.'

'Try Dobson's. He fixed my Raleigh a treat when I smashed it up. Drunk I was. Collided with the Arndale Centre. Didn't even see it.'

'The umpire is a bastard, the umpire is a bastard,' sang the ten-year-old Lancashire supporter when one of his team was given out LBW.

'Watch you language, I said,' shouted Jim and took his shirt off as the sun came out again.

I found Dobson's. Components from a hundred bicycles lay scattered over the entire floor space. An oily individual with a crankshaft clutched in his teeth rose from the sea of metal. I showed him my brake bits and he said:

'Aye, I can find you some of 'em.' He surveyed the mess surrounding him. 'Might take a while, though.'

'It's all right, I'll wait.'

'A couple of weeks I was thinking more in the region of.'

*

Whenever I remember Manchester I see Nurse Grimes handing me a plate of roughage and saying: 'Here. I've just made a high fibre meal,' and we'd sit down with something unrefined on our laps and as we ate she'd talk about what we were going to have for supper. It was one of the first Northern traits I'd been able to identify.

'Why is it that Northerners can't eat one meal without thinking about the next?'

'Why is it that Southerners are so remiss when it comes to defurring their kettles.'

One morning, I was sitting watching the front load automatic when she said: 'I've got the day off, do you want to go and have a look at Marks and Spencers?'

'No thanks.'

'Better still. We could go to Blackpool. We always used to go to Blackpool for our holidays.' And so she made some high fibre banana sandwiches, took a box of Milk Tray she'd been given by My Mrs Williamson (under treatment for hirsutism) and put on some ridiculous pink shoes, and we drove down the M62 to the coast. 'By the way,' she said. 'It always rains in Blackpool.'

But it did more than just rain. This was Blackpool in the Monsoon season. The top of the tower was lost in cloud. Like snowcapped peaks the waves lined up out at sea to rush in and smash themselves to bits against the promenade. The illuminations swung and rattled from lamp-posts and anyone out on the front was wrapped up in plastic, head to toe, dodging fish. Most people had given the day up as lost as soon as they'd got up and were encamped in the amusement arcades or the bars where they danced the conga and sang the Birdie Song until they passed out.

We sat down to dressed crab and a pot of tea in Robert's Oyster Bar on the front, an oasis of wood-panelling and alcoves amongst the barns of plastic and neon. A sign inside said Est. 1876, and these dining rooms were a dim reminder of the days when Blackpool was an entertainment centre that drew the greats. Chaplin performed here, as did W.C. Fields, Houdini, Garbo and Coward. And from all over the North West entire factories would come for their wakes week, the highlight of their year. Blackpool had three grand piers and a copy of the Eiffel tower, and for one week it was full of your mates. Nowadays, people came in their cars in groups of four and they moaned about the weather and said they wished they'd gone to the Greek islands and the town looked unbelievably miserable.

'I know,' said Nurse Grimes, 'let's go to Fleetwood on a tram.'

The tram rattled along the promenade past the golf courses and the very guest house where the Grimes family used to stay. 'It doesn't look any different really,' she said. 'Except they've had the roof fixed and put in a solarium.'

Fleetwood was a few miles up the coast and was once a large and important fishing port, with a once large and important fishing industry which would appear now to have dwindled to a kippers-by-post operation. In fact, the fleet of in-shore vessels is tucked away up the mouth of the River Wyre, but what makes Fleetwood of interest is the lay-out of the town. Designed by Decimus Burton in the 1840s, it is a fine example of early town planning. The streets were said to have been laid out by a plough and they are wide and airy and the traffic flow is good. The old Euston Hotel and the lighthouse have a functional simplicity; the terraces are practical. Fleetwood could be a long lost ancestor of Milton Keynes.

We went into the Lighthouse cafe. 'I'll have some chips,' said Nurse Grimes.

'I'll have a scone,' I said.

'Scone and chips it is then,' said the waitress.

I wrote a job lot of postcards and Nurse Grimes gazed out of the steamed up window. 'Look,' she said, 'there's Marks and Spencers,' and then we were back in the car speeding inland along the motorway with the wipers slapping and the radio going on about a ferret called Mountbatten that someone had found in the Arndale and would the owner like to claim it.

'When I was younger Blackpool seemed a lot bigger,' said Nurse Grimes. 'And of course the summers were a lot warmer and sunnier then as well.'

Next morning it was still raining and we decided not to get up. Only the brainwave of making a blackcurrant and apple crumble got us out of bed.

We sat under the duvet with rivulets running down the windows eating the crumble and watching the Second Test Match. It felt so luxurious I wanted to tell someone. I phoned my script-writing partner, Dick:

'Dick! Guess what. I'm under a duvet with a nurse eating blackcurrant and apple crumble and watching the Test Match.'

'That's amazing, so am I. Are you in Lapland yet?'

Lapland? I hadn't thought about Lapland in days. I'd even neglected my Norwegian study since I'd arrived in Manchester. I looked out of the window at the wet road. I'd leave tomorrow.

'Explain cricket to me,' said Nurse Grimes, as the players left the pitch due to bad light.

'It's easy. There are two sides; they both take it in turns to bat ... '

'I think we'll have a tuna fish bake tonight. Or maybe I'll take some kidney bean casserole out of the freezer.'

' ... and then to bowl, and the side that scores most runs, wins. Easy.'

'I've got some lentils. I could do a lentil roast. Or maybe stuff some peppers. Do you know, I once had a friend who used to stuff carrots.'

I considered this. 'Life's too short to stuff carrots,' I said and got up.

'Where are you going?'

'*Vil de vaere sa snill a fylle batteriet med destillert vann,*' I said. Which I thought meant:

'I need to buy some new brakes.'

But in fact meant:

'Can you fill the battery with distilled water?'

I went back to the shop in Old Trafford. Mr Dobson was up a ladder with a tyre round his neck, and a pair of handlebars stuffed down his waistband.

'Any luck with those brakes,' I asked.

He stepped down. 'Not yet.'

'I need them urgently.'

'Where are you off to?'

'Lapland.'

'Lapland, eh? Is that the place where you get those ornamental reindeer hatstands?'

'That's the place.'

'Aye, you'll need brakes if you're going to up there. Tell you what I can do, I can adapt a pair of Mercury Zenith's. They should stop you. But just in case, I can let you have an Eindhoven Clanger.'

'What's an Eindhoven Clanger?'

'It's an exceedingly loud bell.'

Next morning Nurse Grimes gave me a loaf of homemade bread and a box of Black Magic (Mrs Besant: clot on leg) and watched me pack up my bike. I hadn't seen much of Manchester while I'd been there, but then I've always found big cities make more sense if you pick one area and try to get to know that well, rather than run around in an effort to become vaguely acquainted with the whole.

And I had got to know that little flat better than most visitors. I knew the kitchen intimately. Of the tumble dryer

I could have written the definitive biography. In the
bathroom, I had found corners few travellers can ever have
seen. And as far as the area between the digital alarm clock
and the creeping fig potplant was concerned, I was an
expert. I had some very happy times by the book shelf and by
the Robert Palmer records and I particularly liked that
corner between the Mother-in-Law's Tongue and the
laundry basket. Now it was time to leave it was like starting
the trip all over again, and I felt suddenly very homesick.

'You must come down south sometime,' I said.

'If I do I'm bringing my own water,' said Nurse Grimes.
She stood in the doorway as I strapped on my luggage: 'Are
you really going to Lapland?'

'Yes.'

'Why?'

'For charity.'

'What charity?'

'Aids research.'

'You must be barmy going on your own.'

Over the last two weeks travelling alone had become so
second nature to me, the thought of making this trip
accompanied had ceased to occur. I didn't particularly like
the ephemeral quality of every friendship and even every
conversation, nor times like this when I was leaving the
familiar and the comfortable for the unfamiliar and the
uncomfortable, but I couldn't contemplate any other
arrangement.

'Why don't you come with me, then?' I said.

But all she said was: 'Just remember to look after your
bowels. You Southerners aren't as bowel-conscious as you
ought to be.'

And then I set off through the early morning city. It was
Sunday, and the streets were quiet apart from the gangs of
road workers attacking the tarmac with pneumatic drills.

*

It was strange to be back on my bike again, stranger still with the new brakes I'd fitted. The Mercury Zenith adaptations turned out to be lumps of rubber the size of basketball shoes attached to the old holders. They stopped the bike all right, but each time I braked was like throwing out an anchor; most of that morning I spent climbing down from the handlebars.

But it was my new bell that really excited me. I'd tried it once in Nurse Grimes's flat and it sounded like a fire alarm. I was just waiting for the opportunity to use it in aggression: some Ford Sierra cutting me up, a toxic load not giving way, a farm dog snapping at my heels, an unattentive pedestrian with shopping, any hindrance to my progress would get the full force of the Eindhoven Clanger.

But then after a few miles Manchester seemed an age away and I slipped into a familiar pattern. The wildlife was as squashed as everywhere else (although growing more exotic. I saw my first flattened toad on the A6033 to Todmorden); the radio was still playing hits from the year Kennedy was assassinated, Ronan point collapsed and the Onedin Line began on TV; and there were the familiar roadside distractions, the cigarette ends and drink cans discarded by motorists that were forever bouncing off my head and piling up on the verge, and of course the advertisements, those great displays that you flash past subliminally in a car but which become enormous story boards from a bicycle: vast fingers with manicured nails point at you; huge Big Brother faces with brilliant teeth stare hypnotically from above; crunchie bars take on whole meanings when they're twenty foot long. One poster made me stop it looked so unnerving. And then I realised why. The man posing in the picture was Robert, a friend who did some part-time modelling. The ad was for some savings scheme and there he was staring down at me with a silly grin giving me investment advice. The four sheets that made the whole weren't quite aligned correctly and his face was contorted. I stood in front of it, laughing. It was the first time on the trip I wished I'd brought a camera with me.

Every lawnmower in Calderdale was at work that day and the lawns were show grounds in front of each house that said as much about the owners as their cars or the depth of pile on their living room carpets. There was the two tone effect achieved with precision by the little bald man in Todmorden with his petrol driven Atco. There was the traditional short back and sides lovingly created by the hand driven Mountfield in Mytholmroyd. There was the modernist circular look that the fellow in shorts and I Ran The World t-shirt in Eastwood managed to get with his Flymo. And there was the cricket pitch effect produced by the man in Hebden Bridge on his postage stamp. He rode up and down astride a sit-on mower that resembled a motorbike with rollers, and each time he reached the edge of the lawn he made a three point turn.

But the smell of grass cuttings was aromatic, and with the rowan trees in fruit and the rose bushes crammed with colour, it felt as though summer was full and fat, and I slipped into a cycling stupor, brought round only by an enormous advert for the Gas Board featuring a Sunday roast and an oven ... Balls! I'd forgotton all about my oven. But surely after I put the phone down and switched off the immersion and got the dessert spoons from the kitchen drawer, I turned it off then, because I can remember being in the bathroom earlier and seeing the window open and thinking I'd better go round the flat and close all the windows, and then going into the kitchen and seeing the oven on and switching ... or was it the electricity I switched off, no hang on, after the bathroom I didn't go into the kitchen, I went and wrote a letter to the newsagents to cancel ... oh no! I just remembered. This morning before I left Manchester I made some toast at Nurse Grimes's flat and I left the grill on, I'm sure I did. Yes, I remember I took the toast out and ate it as I was packing. And she was going straight to work after I left. She'd get home tonight to a smouldering ruin ... Just a minute, was that Nell Gwyn and Henry VIII I passed back there?

I looked back and sure enough there were Nell Gwyn and Henry VIII, walking at a pace and pushing a pram. Then a mile or two further I passed a chambermaid from 'Upstairs Downstairs' and a couple of plague victims pushing a supermarket trolley. And not long after that as I called in at a roadside snackbar, Gladstone asked me if I had a light. He eventually got one off Sir Francis Drake who had stopped for a hot chocolate and a Penguin.

'Would you like to donate?' said Dick Turpin, shoving a collection tin under my nose. They were all raising funds for the local Rotoract Club: this was their annual charity walk. Collecting en route was something I could have done if I'd been better organised. Unfortunately, a tin marked 'Money for a good cause, but I can't remember which one,' didn't have the hallmark of authenticity. I put ten pence in Dick Turpin's tin just as a caveman arrived on the scene accompanied by Tonto who slumped down on a stone wall and said: 'I'm not pushing that wheelbarrow no more until I've had a bacon butty.'

Calderdale was millstone grit country, the Pennine building stone that really sounds like the stuff industrial heartlands are made of. And every brick in every building in every town and village was stained black from the soot coughed up by a textile industry that had had its heyday a hundred years previously, but had yet to have its spirit exorcised from these dales. Smokeless fuels had eventually stopped the rot and the towns had been tidied up, but no-one attempted to scrub the houses. The very idea of it was contemptible, one clean exterior in a row of terraces just showed up the mucky ones.

As it was, these Pennine mill communities had a retired

expression. Most of them had become ghost towns when the slump came and the mills closed with no compensation for the workers. In Hebden Bridge asbestos poisoning had infected the town and crippled it. In fact that was what this whole valley of weather-gnarled hills looked like, a victim of industrial disease. Only the decision to remarket the area under the flag of Industrial Heritage had resuscitated it. Ten years ago Hebden Bridge had degenerated to a hippy squat, property could be bought for next to nothing, now the old mills have been converted into industrial units and the town is full of craft shops and estate agencies and been renamed The Pennine Centre.

I sat in a park and had the last of Nurse Grimes's high fibre sandwiches and watched a vintage car rally. A man with a limp sold me a raffle ticket (first prize a set of fitted sheets from Littlewoods) and when quizzed about the mills he assured me that no matter how it might appear, the textile industry still employed the majority of local people, although wages were pitifully low. He said he'd worked in mills once but: 'People don't wear nice flannels any more. They wear things like that,' and he eyed my Al's Garage sapphire blue pullover with the black fleck as if it had been singlehandedly responsible for the downfall of the British textile industry.

'I can remember waking up each morning and knowing what day it was by the density of smoke in the sky,' he said. 'The smog would get thicker and thicker as the week progressed and it would always rain on a Friday.'

I continued through these straggled villages, sharing the road with pristine pre-war Austins. I almost used my Eindoven Clanger for the first time in Nazebottom when a vicar strolled across the road reading the *People*. But I didn't think it was very respectful to ring a bicycle bell at vicars. Beside the poor man had enough problems with his declining congregation. It had reduced him to sticking a sign up outside his church that read: 'CH..CH. What's missing? UR.'

The fact was on a muggy Sunday afternoon most of his parish had been in the pub until closing time and were now sleeping off their lunch in the local recreation ground, an infectious passtime and I found myself pedalling lazily from park bench to park bench. In Sowerby Bridge I watched a game of tennis played by four individuals with all the intensity of a Wimbledon doubles match, the only differences being that Wimbledon players don't play in jeans, their rackets aren't made in Pakistan, they never fart on the court or smoke between games, and they always have at least one rally per game of more than three shots.

Then later I lay on the grass and watched some kids play a five-a-side football match, their play hampered by a punctured ball and a Brownie brass band in the middle of the pitch. The Brownies marched up and down in formation, playing the theme from 'Dallas', only to have a muddy football land amongst them and some equally muddy kids pierce their ranks with well-timed sliding tackles.

'Ought to be bloody well stopped, that,' said a man in a raincoat, and he was right, the Brownie band was dreadful, hopelessly out of tune, out of time and out of step. The football on the other hand was quite skilful, although, a frightening reminder of how near the start of the new season was.

Without realising it I'd slipped easily into Yorkshire and the roads all led into the densely populated conurbation that spread east from the Pennine chain. My way ahead seemed riddled with motorways and I picked up a road map to help navigate a route through. But I was soon lost and heading in the wrong direction, i.e. south. In a moment of incompetence, totally at odds with the Arctic Explorer image I was trying to cultivate, I had misread Halifax for Huddersfield. But maps do this sort of thing to me, I knew that.

In the village of Meltham I asked directions from the only human being I could find in the street, a girl aged about thirteen. It was a stupid thing to do. She dropped the scooter she was playing on and looked at me and said nothing. I smiled and she shied away. Then a window opened, a voice called her into the house, and a mother's face looked out at me with disgust poorly disguised as suspicion. I knew instantly what she was thinking. All summer the newspapers and the radio had been full of stories of the disappearance of children, of children suffering sexual abuse, of little bodies wrapped in bundles dumped on waste ground. It was sad and sickening and I felt a knot in my stomach, but I knew I should never approach children in the street like that again.

In the end I asked in Woody's, a lonely newsagents specialising, according to the doorsign, in the sale of tobacco, newspapers, sweets and footwear. But Woody, bless him, I don't think really knew where he lived, and as the sun set I was still climbing up tortuous hills towards the village of Holmfirth where I decided I was knackered and found myself a Bed and Breakfast.

The house was called Capri and was owned by a couple from the South. They were full of Northern sayings, the sort you find printed on tea towels, and they seemed to be trying to impress upon me what good Northerners they were.

'Close the door after you, or you won't feel the benefit,' she said.

'Aye, there's nowt so queer as folk,' he said.

'Well I'll go to Fleetwood on a tram,' I said, when they asked me for money in advance.

He sat me down in the 'parlour' and took out a pen and paper. 'Right. Breakfast. Cooked, or cereal and toast?'

'Cooked please.'

'Cooked.' He ticked the pad. 'Egg, bacon and fried bread or two boiled eggs?'

'Egg, bacon and fried bread, please.'

'Toast or bread?'

'Toast.'

'Tea or coffee?'

'Tea.'

'Jam or marmalade?'

'What?'

'Jam or marmalade? We have to know. We have to get organised, you see.'

'I don't know. Jam!'

'Apricot or strawberry?'

'Got any blackcurrant?'

'No, just apricot or strawberry'

'I'll have marmalade, then.' He looked at me, thought: troublemaker, eh! and put a thick line through jam and ticked marmalade.

'Marmalade. Lime or Orange?'

'Orange.'

'Thickcut or Golden Shred?'

'You're joking?'

'Aye, you're right I'm joking. We ran out of thickcut this morning. Still.' He dotted his pad. 'That's about it. You're upstairs, first on the left, room one.'

I turned to go. Just as I reached the door he said, 'Oh, nearly forgot, would you like to sit by the window or by the fireplace?'

I went upstairs, dumped my stuff and came back down immediately. I needed a drink. Before going out I knocked on the kitchen door.

'Aye lad? Come straight in; no need to stand on ceremony in this house.'

I went in. He was sitting there in braces by the fire, smoking a pipe, trying desperately to look like Andy Capp.

'I've changed my mind,' I said. 'I'd like two boiled eggs, coffee instead of tea, and apricot jam. Thanks. See you later. Oh, and one more thing, I think I'd like to sit by the fireplace rather than the window.'

*

Next day was Yorkshire Day. In nearby Barnsley a commemorative Yorkshire pudding was baked, the biggest ever. It was 'the size of a carpet' and duly earned its place in the Guinness Book of Records, then it was chucked in the bin. I lay in bed listening to the rest of the news, most of it concerning the floods in the South. Then Chris de Burgh and his lady in red came on. I knew the words by heart, and what had started as a troubadour's melodic declaration of love was fast turning into a mawkish dirge. Halfway through even my radio got fed up with it and its batteries packed up.

Holmfirth was a town that simply couldn't believe its luck. It was just another decaying mill community until fourteen years ago when scriptwriter Roy Clarke submitted a comedy to the BBC featuring three pensioners reliving their childhood with a mischief and sense of humour inspired by Yorkshire. The programme was entitled 'Last of the Summer Wine' and Holmfirth was cast as the location. As the series took off, was repeated and went to further series, and Compo and Foggy and Nora Batty became household names, Holmfirth became a place of pilgrimage, and the show spawned a local industry. Shops in the town began to stock souvenirs bearing images of the programme's stars. The Wrinkled Stocking Cafe, named after Nora Batty's swaddled legs, opened for business. Visitors came by the busload and in their honour Holmfirth council splashed out on a new set of public conveniences.

I bought a postcard with Compo's Wellies on the front, sat in Sid's Cafe and wrote: 'By the time you get this I'll be in Lapland.' – In which case, I thought, I'd better put a second class stamp on it. Then I walked out of the town on the Wakefield Road. A woman and a kid on a tricycle blocked the path ahead. I was still waiting for the chance to use my Eindhoven Clanger for the first time, but it didn't seem right when I wasn't even riding my bicycle. 'Excuse me,' I said instead, and as I brushed past the kid stuck his tongue out and zapped me with a ring from his Dan Dare bell.

A thin rain fell, and the lights on in kitchens at midday gave these dales a look of winter. In one village I took shelter in a library that glowed with electricity. It was empty but for a librarian crouched beneath her desk. I stood there, damply steaming, and she jumped when she saw me and dropped her stamper. I decided to give her my Rocester approach:

'Good afternoon. This is my first time in ... in ... ' here I looked around, trying to glean some sort of clue as to which branch library this was, ' ... in ... in ... in this village, and I want to learn everything there is to know about the place in the time it takes to stop raining.'

She smiled and took her glasses off: 'You don't know where you are, do you?'

'Haven't a clue. I'll take a guess. Wakefield?'

'No.'

'I give up then.'

'You're in Denbigh Dale,' and her face lit up with pride as she led me to the local history section. She'd been waiting all her career for someone like me to walk in.

'Denbigh Dale is renowned for its commemorative pies,' she said and launched into an account of how on special occasions, such as the Silver Jubillee in 1977, the village makes an enormous pie, feet deep and yards across. A special baking tin and oven are commissioned from the steel works. Dozens of sheep and cattle, flocks of chickens and assorted game make up the ingredients, and folk come from miles around to taste the result. A pie had been planned for the royal wedding this summer, but: 'The pie committee uhmmed and arhed and in the end they sent a telegram instead.'

She sat me down in front of a pile of books. On one occasion it appeared 100,000 people turned up at the feast and when the pie was taken out of the oven it was trampled underfoot in the rush. More concerning though were the number of occasions the pie had been improperly cooked in the middle and most of those who tasted a piece had left clutching their stomachs.

Two women with shopping came in from the rain and busied themselves in Romantic Fiction. Outside, the traffic passed with a hushed slosh. In a back room a child's hands ran up the scales of a piano. From somewhere I was sure I could smell a pie being cooked. And I sat there surrounded by books, feeling wonderfully cosy, all I wanted was a story that would help me escape from a wet Monday in South Yorkshire. I plucked out a faded volume from High Adventure: *Moby Dick*, perfect, and I settled down in a comfy chair.

Opposite the title page an elderly hand had written:

'I remember when I was a little girl seeing a whale in the harbour of Cullercoats in Northumberland, then a small fishing village. My father, a gunner, went to Newcastle for military purposes during the summer and my mother and we five children took lodgings for the holiday at Cullercoats.

'The whale, – I think it was called a bottle nose – entered the harbour and the men went out in their small boats and harpooned it. We saw it all very clearly.

'When the whale was dead it was hauled up onto the beach where it looked immense, though it was supposed to be a small species. After a few days it smelt dreadful. I don't know what happened to it. This might have been about 1890.'

A charming introduction, although for setting the mood of the book Herman Melville's is even better: 'Call me Ishmael. Some years ago – never mind how long precisely – having little or no money in my purse, and nothing particular to interest me on shore, I thought I would sail about a little and see the watery part of the world. It is a way I have of driving off the spleen, and regulating the circulation … ' Just like me on my bike really.

'Are you going to slimmers' tonight?' said one of the women in Romantic Fiction to her friend. She was trying to whisper and yet her whispers were louder than normal speech. 'Maureen's going to teach us those get-ready-for-your-bikini exercises.'

' … Whenever I find myself growing grim about the mouth; whenever it is a damp, drizzly November in my soul; whenever I find myself pausing involuntarily in front of coffin warehouses, and bringing up the rear of every funeral I meet … '

'I'd rather spend my time in the solarium,' said another voice from Romantic Fiction.

'In the what?'

'In the solarium. You know, that false sun.'

'Gives you cancer that does.'

'It's losing weight that gives you cancer.'

'It's only getting ready for bikini exercises.'

' … and especially whenever my hypos gets such an upper hand of me, that it requires a strong moral principle to prevent me from deliberately stepping into the street, and methodically knocking people's hats off … '

'I'll be ready for my bikini if I go under the solarium for a couple of sessions. You go brown in ten minutes or something.'

'Where are you going to wear a bikini?'

'Corfu. Hotel Ipsos. Full board. Airport tax, liquor factory excursion and parascending lessons included. Guaranteed no surcharges.'

'I went to Corfu. I couldn't read the menu, it was in Greek, see. "Try this," the waiter said, and he pointed to a meal that had triangles in it. But I was buggered if I was going to eat something I couldn't pronounce. So we went and had this Greek ethnic evening. It was like a competition to see who could eat the most tomatoes.'

' ... then I account it high time to get to sea as soon as I can. This is my substitute for pistol and ball. With a philosophical flourish Cato throws himself upon his sword; I quietly take to the ship.'

'I'm going to Lanzarote myself. It's volcanic, you know.'

I couldn't concentrate. I put the book back and left, wishing for Ishmael's conviction.

But their conversation stuck with me as I continued on through the South Yorkshire mining communities, all hotbeds of militancy during the appalling strike of two years previously. A thin scar had formed since but the horizons looked dismal and hopeless. The collieries that hadn't been closed rose out of the slag heaps like groaning dinosaurs, a thin black film of dust covering everything from miners to lollypop ladies; the drizzle finishing the scene off exactly. And amongst it all, a string of beauty salons offering ultra-violet sessions, bucket travel shops offering two weeks in Torremolinos for thirty-five pence, and sooty video shops with lurid posters plastered across the windows advertising 'The Return of The Lust Vampires'. They were flagrant escape routes, the cheapest and most immediate.

Later that day I came across the largest breaker's yard I'd ever seen, a graveyard of buses and trucks and cars, piles of pummelled metal, rusting away. And then not far away I heard the steady throb of heavy traffic through the trees and I couldn't understand it as I was on a quiet lane, but then suddenly, there was the M1, a well camouflaged stream of gleaming company cars, National Buses and Long Vehicles with number plates from all over Europe. I stood on the bridge awhile and watched as The Paxo Rooster Booster went under followed by Hull Cesspool Emptying Service Ltd. and Jesswell's Human Cannonball Act. As I'd come up the country I'd passed over a number of motorways, all unexpectedly like this, and each time they reminded me of arteries, and the traffic was a drug pumped up and down the trunk of the country at an addictive rate.

I was about to pedal off when a moaning great yellow thing rolling along on a couple of dozen wheels and plastered with words like, 'Highly Inflammable, Corrosive, Keep a Safe Distance, Collide With Me And Its Curtains Sunbeam', came steaming round the corner like a wild animal and thundered towards me. I shouted and waved but the beast didn't deviate. In desperation I reached for the Eindhoven Clanger. I flicked the lever once and the scene slipped into slow motion. Birds flew from trees. Windows opened in distant houses. In a pub a mile away the landlord called time. The juggernaut screeched to a halt.

The driver wound his window down. 'Which way's London mate?'

I pointed towards to the southbound carriageway. A sign read, London 170 miles. It had taken me almost three weeks to get this far. My efforts suddenly seemed pathetic. It was the middle of August already and Lapland was still over a thousand miles away. The midnight sun was slowly sinking. It was time I got a move on.

5. The Yorkshire Dales: What to Wear

I set out for Bradford on the morning of the Glorious Twelfth. The first grouse in Britain had been shot at dawn on Alston Moor by Bob Slack of Cumbria. My stars for the day were: 'Good day for being the life and soul of the party, don't let crotchety people pull you down with their misery and groans'. The grouse's stars were: 'Bad day for flying over Alston Moor, keep well clear of the people called Bob Slack'.

I was passing through rugby league country. The names on the signposts were familiar but only from Grandstand when some flat-capped commentator would stand in the middle of a field and in an accent reminiscent of someone breathing helium, list those legendary homes of the Up an' Under: Castleford, Featherstone, Pontefract, Wakefield. In Wakefield I passed right by the ground and slipped inside for a look. Wakefield Trinity has always had a rather more venerable reputation than the other clubs, an air of glamour even, but the stadium was like a cracked shell, a collection of battered sheds strewn with lumps of concrete. Maybe that was the sort of ambience a successful rugby league club strived for.

A mystery voice was on Radio Pennine. I wasn't sure if it was Tim Brooke-Taylor or Petula Clarke. But my mind was on other things. I was cycling on main roads, and I needed all my concentration to avoid the trucks that clipped my ears with their wing mirrors. In fact of late, the weather and the traffic had highlighted the inadequacies of my equipment. Rainwear would have been useful. A suit of armour would have been best. In the section What To Wear in my bicycle book, the importance of the correct attire was dealt with at length and useful tips were given, such as what sort of gloves should be worn to best reduce vibration from handlebars – somewhere, it probably even gave instructions on how to put them on: 'put hand through hole A and fingers through holes B, C, D, E and F.'

The mystery voice was still puzzling Radio Pennine listeners:

'It's Gordon Honeycombe,' said Bernard Nesbitt a panel beater from Dewsbury.

'I'm convinced it's Brian Clough,' said Mrs E Rooney, mother of two from Shipley.

'It's that man with the bowtie on the telly,' said Angela Arkwright, a telephonist from Elland who would like to say hello to her Mum and Dad, sister Fiona, boyfriend Tim, cat Ninelives and anyone else who knows her.

'It is without a shadow of a doubt – and you're going to laugh at this Tony – but it really does sound just like the lad who works behind the counter at Dewhurst's in town,' said Ken from Batley.

I was in Batley at the time, in fact I cycled right past Dewhurst's and I would have gone in and checked Ken's theory but it was half day closing, and anyway I was convinced now that the mystery voice was Bernard Cribbens, so convinced I stopped at a phone box to call Radio Pennine but the coin box had been smashed, the cord cut and the receiver mouthpiece melted where someone had tried to burn the kiosk to the ground.

I walked round Batley looking for the Post Office and I decided I liked the town. But I was beginning to think this was a failing of mine. I seemed to like almost everywhere. I remember some people in Manchester talking about neighbouring Stockport as if the place was so wretched it should have been dismantled, and yet what I'd noticed when I'd passed through there had been cobbled streets and viaducts. I said I'd found Stockport pretty, and no-one could believe me.

And sometimes I couldn't believe myself. But I really did find Batley pleasant, and Wakefield and Halifax and all those fabled names traditionally synonymous with Northern grit. Batley was the sort of location comedians used in jokes. ('I'm not saying my mother-in-law's ugly but she comes from Batley'). Yet approaching there – as with most of these Pennine towns, over the brow of a hill – and looking down over the whole, the scene was hardly gloomy. You expected a choked environment, always twilight, cars with their lights on even during the day, everything from fingernails to wet pavements ingrained with factory soot. But what you got was fields sloping off hills into town centres where you found standard flower tubs, amorphous precincts and one-way systems, with a gleaming job centre always the brightest window in the high street. These towns looked polished and primed to go to work. Unfortunately, there was little work to go to.

I've always been a fan of the postal service. The very concept of the Royal Mail I find miraculous. No matter where I am in the world I can send Christmas Greetings to my Aunt Dorothy in Aylesbury and vice versa. The technology behind such an operation, like that of aeroplanes, telephones, automatic kettles and electric toothbrushes, has me in awe, and I get annoyed when people complain of such peccadillos as lost letters, smashed parcels, sealed pillar boxes, and terrorist postmen. I don't even mind queues in the post office.

In Batley, however, folk aren't so easily impressed.

The queue seemed about the normal size to me, only about fifteen people, but the manager had ensured it would quickly grow to a respectable length by allocating staff to only two of the six windows. We're used to this sort of thing in my local office. You join a queue for a eighteen pence stamp and you accept that by the time you reach the window it will cost nineteen. But in Batley they're a militant lot. They stood there with their teeth clenched, hats pulled down and coats buttoned agains the August chill. Conversation was terse.

'I've only come down here to buy a postal order to send to our Jeffrey in New Zealand,' said Mrs Poulson, a pinched woman with a Spar carrier bag.

'Do you know you can get Aids from licking stamps,' said Eric Thorogood, a retired off-licensee come to pick up a road tax application form.

I stood at the back minding my own business, but then I remembered my stars, something about me being the life and soul of the party wasn't it? Not allowing crotchety people to get me down with their misery or something. So I said to Mrs Poulson: 'Do you know anywhere in town where I can buy some cycling plus-twos? Ideally they should be worsted and have a reinforced seat.' She looked at me and I knew she wanted to make some comment about my pullover, but at that point one of the two remaining windows slammed shut and the assistant disappeared and Mrs Poulson decided enough was enough.

'This is supposed to be a main post office, is this,' she shrieked, 'and there's only one window open and it's the same every week and we've had all we can take, isn't that so Eric?'

'Aye, we've had all we can take,' said Eric.

'I've only come down here to buy a postal order to send to my Jeffrey who's over in New Zealand and doing very well for himself as a breakfast chef, and I've had to wait twenty minutes.'

'Aye, twenty minutes,' said Eric.

'And Eric here has had to wait just as long for his road tax application form and he's driven here all the way from Tavistock Rd with a tax-applied-for disc sellotaped to his windscreen.' Here Mrs Poulson gesticulated with her Spar bag.

'You tell them Mrs Pouslon,' said a man with sandals and socks on, 'you tell them I've got to licence my TV and if it's not licenced on time BBC 2 goes funny. And I'm not putting a licence-applied-for sticker on the screen neither, it's only an eighteen inch as it is.'

The manager appeared and tried to look calm but Mrs Poulson reduced him to a flaming lump of embarrassment in minutes.

'I've got staff problems,' he pleaded.

'My Jack'll work for you,' said a lady behind me with a Freeman Hardy Willis bag.

'My staff are off sick,' said the manager, 'it's Mrs Sparrow, she's poorly.'

The queue was struck by a sudden wave of remorse. 'Mrs Sparrow?' said Mrs Poulson, 'It's not her side is it?'

'Aye, it's her side,' said the manager.

'Oh, I am sorry to hear that. Did you hear, everyone? Doreen Sparrow's not well.'

'Her side is it?' said the lady with the Freeman Hardy Willis bag.'

'Aye, it's her side,' said Mrs Poulson, who had now jumped about ten places and was by the window. 'Give me a thirty bob postal order, and a stamp to Cookton's Drive, Timaru, near Christchurch, New Zealand. And have you got the automatic licker handy? I don't want any Aids, ta very much.'

'The Sound of Music' was about to begin its summer run at the Alhambra theatre in Bradford, but there was already a smell of Autumn in the air. I freewheeled down hills into the sirens and bus fumes of the city centre, and began to feel the familiar evening chill that seemed to sit in these Pennine valleys each night. The sky was purple and I began to think of The Yorkshire Ripper.

The first thing I noticed in Bradford was the pistachio-and-cream buses after the vivid orange-and-white of Manchester. And then there was the magnificent Italianate town hall, a building that you'd have placed in Florence or Siena but for the gallery of sculptures of every English sovereign from William the Conqueror to Victoria lining the facade.

But Bradford isn't really much to look at. Instead, it's the visitor's sense of smell that the city grabs hold of and pins against the wall. As I cycled up the Great Horlton Rd every building I passed shouted, hello! to my nose. I was entering the Asian district of the city, a milieu of curry houses, Asian sweet shops and delicatessens that bombard your nostrils with different degrees of pungency on every street corner. One minute saffron, the next mint, the next coriander. Curried aromas seep out through every crack and set the saliva ducts pumping. The place is a nasal orgasm.

I had an address to call on in Bradford, a teacher and a social worker who lived in the heart of the Asian community. They rented a back-to-back, two rooms, one up one down. As soon as I arrived Frank said: 'Coming for a walk?'

A few months previously his girlfriend Susan had banned smoking in the house and Frank had to put his jacket on and disappear outside whenever he felt the nicotine urge. To begin with, he stood out in the yard, but: 'As soon as I lit up, all the Hindus came out and tried to bum fags off me.'

So Frank began to walk as he smoked; to begin with just around the block a few times but then he began to wander. He explored the Asian community properly; he got to know the old industrial quarter of the city, the horizons of redundant textile mills. When I arrived he was up to about twenty walks a day and he couldn't work out if smoking was making him healthier or walking was giving him bronchitis. More important though, he knew the city like the back of a Silk Cut packet; that evening we just went for a quick dimp but the following morning he took me out for a proper smoke.

The origins of Bradford's Asian community can be traced directly back to the days when the textile industry thrived. The popular view is that their immigration was the result of a desire for cheap labour, whereas in fact, it was directly due to the mill barons' decision to re-equip their mills with new machinery, and the realisation that to make their investment pay they would have to work it 24 hours a day. The night shift found few volunteers, mill work was traditionally badly paid, and so recruitment began 7000 miles away in Pakistan, around the Punjab, and in Kashmir and Mirpur where in the early 1960s a great dam was built displacing some 100,000 people, compensating them with enough money to afford the fare to Bradford.

At first it was all seen as a temporary influx and was lived with. The aim of this new work force was, surely, simply to make its money and leave. And besides, the immigrants filled undesirable jobs, and houses. But instead of leaving, the workers arranged for their wives and children to come and join them; they didn't return home either when the textile business was hit by the recession in the seventies and tens of thousands of jobs were lost. The non-white population rose to 20%, most of them Muslims, but also Sikhs and Gujerati factions. A high birthrate and a steady trickle of secondary immigrants ensured that numbers increased steadily.

But these immigrants weren't like the Poles or Jews who had come to Bradford after the war and quickly assimilated themselves. The Asians had a culture the white community had trouble absorbing and as mosques began to fill the wasteland left by demolished industry, racial tension grew and inevitably manifested itself in violence.

For the whole morning Frank led me round this Asian quarter. We stood in the checkout queue at the Halal supermarket and sheltered for a while in the Sari Centre which smelt of curried cotton, and was an incongruous splash of eastern mystique against the pale Pennine sky. We wandered up streets full of dark and doe-eyed children and limp washing hanging in the dirty breeze. It looked squalid on the exterior, although amongst it all occasionally there was evidence of personal wealth. A Mercedes perhaps, parked outside a terrace. The truth was many of these families had made fortunes in Bradford but had resisted moving to one of the more salubrious parts of town for fear of racial attacks.

We finished with a meal in the Kashmir, an Asian cafe next door to the city morgue, an ethnic kind of haunt although popular with the sort of whites who roll in at four o'clock on a Saturday morning with ten pints of Tetley's inside them and say: 'Hey, hit me with a hot one.' We had a portion of Pakal Dal, and some chapatti to scoop it up with.

'I like living amongst the Asians,' said Frank. 'They don't go round mugging people. They're much better achievers at school. And they look after their elderly. More industrious people in general, in fact. I really like them. I just wish they'd speak to me now and again.'

But this ethnic tour of Bradford was about to become official. The tourist board had realised the potential in the culture shock of the Asian community and was planning coachtours. The idea of Bradford as a tourist attraction is a fantastic one, and yet the city has managed to market itself thus, winning awards in the process. The Asian tour is the latest innovation, but the real jewel in the crown is the city's industrial heritage, its former glory as the textile centre of the world.

Much of the old mill area is in a state of decay now, a sorry collection of once grandiose buildings surrounded by barbed wire and demolition notices. But Bradford's rebirth has managed to restore some of the evidence of the enormous wealth once generated by wool, particularly down by the Leeds-Liverpool Canal where the empires of the great wool barons were centred in edifices of a couple of million bricks each.

Sir Titus Salt was the man himself. The Italian styled facade of his magnificent mill is reminiscent of a Renaissance palace, and the ornate gardens belie the dirt and sweat that was once generated inside. A statue of Salt in a nearby park gives him a benevolent face, and it seems that as a mill baron he was uncharacteristic in being the proud owner of a big heart, one that cared deeply for the welfare of his employees. In an effort to ensure them a good standard of living he built Saltaire, an estate of industrial housing with schools and libraries nearby to the mill. But this was no ordinary industrial village. Salt wanted an environment for his workers that encouraged rather than oppressed them, and the houses, in keeping with the mill, have the same Italianate form. The whole village has recently been scrubbed of its grime and now looks like a film set, and has become the fashionable place to live in Bradford, particularly if you're a teacher or a social worker. Frank and Susan were in the process of buying one of the cottages and they showed me proudly round.

Frank lit a cigarette. Susan had yet to ban smoking in this house. We gazed out of the stained glass window that looked out over the railway line and the canal and a mill cafe where you could get a Bradford Cream Tea.

Frank blew cigarette smoke through his nose, and said to me: 'Are you really going to Lapland?'

'Yes. I'm really going to Lapland.'

'Why?'

'For charity. Amnesty International.'

'You know it snows there in the summer.'

'No it doesn't.

'Yes it does.'

'It doesn't.'

'Does.'

'Doesn't ... does it?'

'Think so ... mind you, it snows in Bradford some summers.'

'I should get yourself a hat.' said Susan. 'And when you get to Lapland get youself a hatstand, one of those ornamental reindeer horn ones.'

Next morning I called at the Bradford Arndale Centre and bought a hat: – 'A traditional tea-cosy style is perfectly suitable,' said my bicycle book. And some socks:– 'the smart cyclist will wear white ankle socks or knee length patterned stockings,' and a bright yellow cape: – 'the sensible cyclist always carries a brightly coloured waterproof strapped to his saddle or saddlebag'.

I tried the cape on when I got outside; immediately the rain began.

Outside Baildon I stopped in a car park to pump up my tyres. Behind me was the whole of Bradford and its environs, the erstwhile industrial pulse of the nation that was now all rather silent. 'And was Jerusalem builded here among these dark satanic mills' of Bradford, Bingley, Huddersfield, Leeds, Halifax? ... It suddenly dawned on me they were all the names of building societies.

I cycled away. I'd spent too long over the last week in cities and on main roads, but ahead of me now was dale and moorland as far a Newcastle. As I reached the first moor the rain grew heavier:

'*For et fryktelig vaer!*' I shouted.

('What awful weather.')

It didn't really snow in Lapland in the summer, did it?

*

The Lapland terrain is the stage for a constant struggle between man and the considerable forces of nature.

In the southernmost areas are the great coniferous forests, the ancient hunting grounds. Further north are the pine and spruce which eventually give way to the dwarf trees and bushes of the tundra region that stretches all the way up to the Arctic coast, much of it over high ground, particularly in Finnmark and on the Swedish-Norwegian border where the land rises to over 6,000 feet.

It's tough country, and although Lapland is traditionally known as the land of the midnight sun it should always be remembered that this natural delight comes in the same package as the land of the noon moon and that this is predominantly a cold and dark land. The Gulf Stream provides a mild summer but come September, frosts arrive without warning. And then the night falls, winds veer to the north and the east and temperatures drop into the ice age. There's an old folk song the reindeer herdsmen sing around this time:

> When the sun is gone from the purple mountains
> And the reindeer must break the ice to drink from
> Squirrel Lake.
> When the spruce trees glisten but look mournful,
> Then will I always wear a hat.*

In Ilkley in West Yorkshire, where the winters aren't exactly of the ice age variety, but can be severe nevertheless, they also have a folk song concerning the foolhardiness of stepping outside without headgear:

> Where hast tha been since I saw thee, I saw thee,
> on Ilkley Moor bar taht.

* Hat songs of Northern Europe, by Helmut Olsen.

Fortunately, I was now suitably attired hatwise. Although, I felt I was going to need rather more than a warm head to navigate me safely through the country I could see in the distance. Ilkley Moor was certainly as bleak as the folk song would have one believe, but even that didn't look anything like as unwelcoming as the fells and dales to the north into which I was heading. In the permanent grey light they resembled the mountains of the moon and if I was going to venture into that lot I'd need supplies. Bananas would do the trick.

On the Leeds Road in Ilkley I found a grocery store. 'Nice day,' said the grocer, gazing out from behind his Outspan mobile. This was a poor joke to make in front of a cyclist. It had rained since Bradford and there was a wind picking up. On the radio that morning even the weatherman had said he was sure the summers were warmer and dryer when he was younger.

I asked for a handful of bananas and said: 'How's business?'

'What business?' asked the grocer. 'I used to be in the centre of the town, I did' and he pointed to the sign above his shop, Central Stores it said. 'Trouble was the whole town went and moved two hundred yards up the road.'

Looking up the road you could see that the commercial centre of Ilkely was now a car park surrounded by a quadrangle of shops. You parked and immediately had easy access to everything you wanted to buy, whilst the Leeds Road, which no doubt used to be a prime location, was now just a race track for juggernauts.

'When I first came here this was a proper shop,' he said and he swung my brown bag of bananas over and twisted the corners in inimitable grocers' style. 'Then they went and put double yellow lines down outside. Double yellows are fatal for any business. Take a look for yourself.' He took me outside; it was true, almost every other shop window on the

Leeds Road had a For Sale notice. It clearly wouldn't be long before Central Stores joined them.

'It's not fair,' said the grocer, 'I've put up a new formica sign. I'm cheaper than those precinct places. I've got a better selection and a good display.'

But he wasn't cheaper than the precinct grocery shops. Nor was his display better. And quite frankly, his new sign just wasn't *avant garde* enough. Formica is a bit *passé* after all. In shopping centres a grocer had to have a stained wood exterior and a name like Juicy Lucy's Fruitery. He had to have an apron with 'hi! my names Cindy and I'm here to serve you,' on the front, and kiwi fruit and mangoes sitting in the window. Calling yourself Central Stores and depending on an Outspan mobile to pull the punters just wasn't good enough any more.

He handed me my bananas: 'You've been eating too many of these.'

'Why do you say that?'

'You're turning yellow, that's why.'

I continued towards Skipton along a main road, the rain beginning to come in squalls. On cue the radio came in with a nostalgia show from the sixties playing songs about long lost summers. I was pedalling along singing: 'It never rains in Southern California', and 'I'm going where the sun keeps shining, though the pouring rain. Going where the weather suits my clothes', whilst the water dripped down my neck. It was all too much for me. I'd reached breaking point and I tossed my head back and cried:

'I'm sure the summers were once warmer and dryer than this. There! I've said it. I admit it. The summers were once definitely better, longer, sunnier, cheaper, safer, the standard of living was higher, folk were nicer to each other, and life in general was of a better quality and everyone was happier, no doubt about it whatsoever...' A truck passed and showered me with its slipstream and forced me into a roadside cafe.

'Bloody lorry drivers!' I said to the assembled clientele. 'They don't feel satisfied unless they've run down their cyclist for the day.' A second or two too late I realised what a *faux pas* any complaint directed at the lorry driving fraternity was in this particular establishment. Through the back window I could see in the lay-by a couple of trailers, a removals van, a petrol tanker and the ubiquitous forty foot long toxic loader, and everyone in the place had overalls with witty motifs like, Runcorn Scrap Metal Ltd., written on the breast pocket.

I tried to take off my cape but I couln't get it over my head so I sat there in it and had a mug of tea and a fried egg sandwich which for some reason was bright yellow on the outside as well as the inside. I felt severely ignored. A shame, it was a good cafe. You could have fried eggs with everything – in fact I think it was compulsory – and every time 'Lady in Red' came on the jukebox a lorry driver kicked it until it went off.

That evening I crossed into the Dales National Park. It had been a long day but apart from the weather, the lorries, the usual battles with killer farm dogs, and the flying creature I'd swallowed just outside Skipton which I was convinced had been a thrush, I'd really enjoyed myself.

And then as I reached Malham the rain suddenly stopped and there was a devil of a sunset. Tonight I would sleep out, I decided, but first I wanted to satisfy the sudden craving I had for Theakston's bitter and two sausages, chips and peas with a sachet of English mustard. I was in luck, that was exactly what was on offer in the village pub.

I sat in the bar and fought to get my cape off, I'd got my head into it, damn it, I could get my head out of it. I wasn't going to wear this thing all through the Mediterranean-like

Lapp summer. I wrestled with it a while but then decided to pretend it was a big napkin.

Malham is a popular watering hole for walkers on the Pennine Way, that infamous two hundred and seventy mile ordeal that follows the backbone of England from Derbyshire to the Scottish border. It's a trek over beautiful and unspoilt upland, but also unpredictable and capable of turning inhospitable with ease. Judging from the wrecks that sat in the corners of the bar that evening, it had been wicked up on the hills that day. A frail chap eating chips with his fingers said to his companion:

'That rain really got me down this afternoon, George.'

'You're not properly equipped, are you?' said George. 'You ought to get some oilskins like my blue ones. Are you going to eat all those chips?'

'Why blue? Does blue repel water or something?'

'Are you going to eat that roll?'

'I mean, I worry sometimes when the clouds roll in. I keep thinking about those people in the Andes plane crash.'

'I could eat that shepherd's pie all over again, you know.'

'They had to eat each other. I mean, I know we're only forty miles from Sheffield, and we've got some tins of John West salmon for emergencies, but ... '

'It's no good I'm going to have one of those pickled eggs. Might have a packet of crisps as well.'

The party on the other side were rather more spiritual:

'What I find marvellous about the Dales, Trevor, about nature in general, is the way everything seems to have its own place.'

'That's quite right. Everything seems to have its own place.'

'And everything seems to have a reason for being there.'

'Everything. There's a reason for everything, I've noticed that.'

'It's just unfortunate we're not privy to what that reason is.'

'Unfortunate, that is.'

'I mean, I was looking at this rock today and I started to think: why is that rock there under that birch tree, instead of over there amongst the heather? And in the end I concluded: that's the wonder of nature, that is.'

'Aye, the wonder of nature.' Trevor pondered on this a while, then said: 'Someone might have thrown it, of course.'

'What?'

'The reason why it was under the birch tree instead of amongst the heather could have been because someone threw it.'

'Threw what?'

'That rock.'

'Don't be so stupid.'

'Yes, of course, you're right, I'm being stupid.'

Two walkers, who really shouldn't have been walking together, were having their evening argument. You got the feeling they spent their days like this as well:

'It's K. A. G. O. O. L.'

'It's not, I know it's not. It's C. A. G. O. U. L. E.'

'It's not. Listen, I've been a rambler a lot longer than you have and I'm telling you it's K. A. G. O. O. L.'

'No, no, you're spelling it phonetically, like a child would. It's C. A. G. O. U. L. E. It comes from the latin, caculla, a monk's cowl.'

'No, I'm sorry, you're wrong. I saw it when I bought mine in Bailey's in Harrogate. There was a whole rack of them and it said "Kagools £18.50". And it was spelt K. A. G. O. O. L.'

'You paid £18.50 for your Cagoule?'

'Aye, what of it?'

'I got exactly the same one for £15.20 in the Bradford Arndale.'

'I got mine in the Bradford Arndale,' I said. 'It's not a Cagoule actually, it's more of a cape, C. A. P. E. cape.'

They both looked at me. 'Do you know you're yellow?' One of them said.

'What?'

'Your face is yellow.'

'Mustard,' I said. Wiping my lips.

'It's on your forehead.'

'I'm a messy eater.'

I sat there wondering if it was really possible to overdose on bananas, until I was distracted by people coming in with dripping heads and sodden boots, and making comments like: 'Strange, it seemed such a nice evening a couple of minutes ago.' I went outside and found my bike standing alone in a downpour, my luggage soaked. I pulled my hood up and walked out of the village and into the pitch black night. I was looking for a hedge or something to crawl under, but I picked out a barn and sat and sheltered there. The night was full of scratching noises and the straining of corrugated metal in the wind and I began to think of a film I'd seen called 'An American Werewolf in London', about two hikers out on the moors in Yorkshire attacked by a werewolf. One's imagination can be really unhelpful at times. Why couldn't it have conjured up memories of 'A Room With A View', which I'd seen with Nurse Grimes in Manchester where the hero sits on a balcony overlooking the Arno in Florence and nibbles the heroine all over?

A thin ray of sunlight pierced my eyes. A songbird sang for the fun of it. A mist crept over the meadow contemplating dissipation. A herd of Jerseys chomped the wet grass, one lowed for the fun of it, another butted her, also for the fun of it. The sunlight grew stronger. It streamed through the wooden slats of the barn. I could hear children laughing and playing outside. They sounded as though they were on a beach. A dog barked, again just for the fun of it. A radio came on and a voice said: 'Warm and sunny with a high of twenty-four degrees. Outlook, the same', and that's when I knew it was a dream.

I woke up in a strange bedroom, the sound of rain pelting on the roof. I'd been in a barn, hadn't I? I'd been sitting there, soaked. Then I'd heard a shrill howl in the distance and I'd run all the way to Mr and Mrs Nugent's Bed and Breakfast Guest House, £7.50 a night, choice of four breakfast cereals:

'We don't get many cyclists here,' Mrs Nugent had said.

'Not yellow ones, any road,' Mr Nugent had said.

I'd run upstairs and looked in the mirror. I was the colour of Flora margarine. I cut the neck of my cape and tore it off. My whole body was yellow. I had advanced banana syndrome. The peculiar thing was I was exactly the same colour as my cape.

A branch cracked outside. I pulled back the curtain and saw a monotone world. The rain had made the colours of the countryside run as well, and the result was a universal greyness.

But limestone looks good in weather like this, greyness becomes it, and the Yorkshire Dales are sculptures in the stuff, a chain of limestone hills, capped with that old friend millstone grit and knitted together by the drystone walls that run across the landscape like seams.

Potholes riddle this rock, waterfalls adorn it, and now and again nature uses it purely to show off. Such is the case with Malham Cove, a three hundred foot high natural amphitheatre, the product of continuous erosion, a work in progress if you like. Over the years this magnificent site has become a place of pilgrimage for naturalists, geologists, artists and caravanners alike, including that doyen of the rambling fraternity, William Wordsworth who visited here on his likelong search for words to rhyme with daffodil.

I remember the cove well because, as with everything else

that weekend that possessed an overhang of any description, I used it to shelter under. I stood there watching the rain stream impressively off the cliff, giving a performance of the process of erosion especially for me.

The real show of the morning, however, I heard before I saw. A piercing whistle was carried to me on the wind. Then a flock of sheep appeared, wheeled round the hillside by a dog that responded to the signals as if on remote control. Behind them all came the shepherd, bent into the wind, hat pulled over his eyes, his boots full of water, and muttering, like a tramp: 'Bastards, they're all bastards, everyone of them's a bloody bastard. I don't have to do this job, you know. Bastards.'

Neither was his dog exactly the well groomed film star you normally see on television. This animal was thin and ugly, and bred for the job. He sprinted up hillsides with the stride of a horse and the swerve of a hare, cajoling and pressurising the sheep, mopping them up and funnelling them towards the field like liquid into a bottle neck.

I watched them work for a while then pushed my bike to the National Park centre and studied the map on the wall, which only confirmed my fears that direct routes through the Dales were few and those that there were were ferociously steep. However, there was an old drover's road that led over the fell above Malham to the hamlet of Kilnsey, and from there it seemed I could follow a B road up into North Yorkshire. I asked the warden if the drover's road could be cycled.

'Yes, yes, no problem. Well, that is to say, not much of a problem. Lots of cyclists do it all the time. Well, some do it anyway. Some do it now and again that is. A few scouts have already come over that way today on bikes. That is to say one scout, and he hasn't arrived yet. But you'll be all right. Should be, anyway.'

With my cape flapping in the wind and the rain beginning

to sting I set off towards Gordale Scar, another magnificent limestone fissure, and if anything more striking than Malham Cove because it appeared unannounced. I continued to climb, then the metalled road petered out. I passed a farmhouse and ahead the grassed track led towards nothing but bleak moorland. The contours of the land around melted in the mist. Clouds hurtled across the sky. The sky hurtled across the sky. I caught glimpses of fells in the distance. It was as if I was trapped in some Viking saga and I got annoyed with myself for wanting to sing Sandie Shaw's 1967 Eurovision Song Contest entry, 'Puppet on a String'. I looked round; the farmhouse had vanished and the horizon disappeared. I could see nothing, not even a sheep. I was pushing a bicycle across an empty moor. I had no map and no food. My specialist equipment consisted of a compass, a knife, fork and spoon set, an enamel plate, a pair of sunglasses with one lens missing, a box of assorted elastic bands, a phone card and a Norwegian phrase book, and I was standing there, mumbling: 'I wonder if one day that you'll say that you care, if you say you love me madly, I'll gladly be there, like a puppet on a string, da, da, dadadada.'

It's funny the things you think of when you're stranded on a moor contemplating your imminent demise. You think how your life might have been different if you'd worked for your Maths O-level, if you'd kept practising the piano, if you'd asked Vanessa Blunden to go with you to the Jethro Tull concert. Then after ten minutes of imminency your demise starts to get more mundane and you start to think of things like the cost of the colour TV licence, how far it is from Norwich to Canterbury via the M25 and how it doesn't really matter now if you left home without turning your oven off or not, – although, thinking about it, it suddenly occurred to me that after I'd gone round the flat closing all the windows and written the note to the newsagents, I collected together the items of immense value I own, things like my 100-yard back stroke certificate, my collection of cup final programmes and my Roy Orbison albums, and put them in a place of safe keeping – which I couldn't now remember, – and it was after that I went back into the kitchen and turned off ... no, the next thing I did was to write a letter to DVLC in Swansea to claim a refund on my road tax, then I remember thinking to myself: 'It's a bit hot in here' and that's when I went back into the kitchen and turned off the oven ... or maybe I didn't.

It was only when I imagined what would happen if instead of perishing I drifted into a coma and was laid out in intensive care on a life support machine that things started to get interesting again. I wondered who would come and visit me. Who'd come and try and talk me round. Nurse Grimes would. She'd bring a box of soft centres (Mrs Tatler: hip replacement,) and she'd sit there eating them all and say things like: 'I told you this sort of thing would happen if you didn't look after your bowels.' Linda would probably breeze in as well and ask the duty nurse if I'd mentioned anything about a bottle of duty free perfume: 'Diorissima, 90ml atomiser. Oh, and if he comes round tell him his oven blew up a few days ago and his flat was levelled.' And Ralph would come in the middle of the night and say: 'That'll teach you to swipe my Sainsburys' cheese and bacon flan.' They might get the England cricket team to record a message of encouragement to play over and over to me. Something like: 'Hi Mark! it's Mike Gatting here. Me and the lads obviously hope that you get better, obviously. And obviously we think that if you work at it hard enough you'll get the right result, that's obvious, obviously.' Or maybe they'd play a record to try to bring me round. The new Paul Simon single, 'You Can Call Me Al!' would do nicely, anything really, apart from Chris de Burgh and his Lady in Red. Hang on! I could hear that now. There it was: 'My Lady in Reeeeeed', coming through the mist. I'd already begun to hallucinate.

Chris de Burgh got louder. Two white lights pierced the grey. A diesel engine moaned and a Landrover came into view with the words Mountain Rescue on the side. I shouted and waved, let my bike tumble and ran over and threw my arms round the vehicle. Chris de Burgh was turned off. The window was wound down and a head with an unlit cigarette in its mouth stuck itself out and said:

'Haven't got a light have you. ... eerg! what's wrong with your face?'

I'd obviously gone yellow again. 'Don't worry it's not contagious,' I said and handed him a sodden box of matches.

He lit his cigarette. 'Mind if I keep them, thanks. Don't suppose you've seen a cyclist round here, have you? We've been sent out to rescue one.'

I said: 'Yes. Me. I'm a cyclist. And I need rescuing.'

'No, sorry mate, we can't rescue you,' said his colleague in the passenger seat. 'See, the cyclist we've been sent out to rescue is a scout. You haven't even got a scout's hat or any badges or anything, have you?' His accent was from London. The driver's was Welsh. In the back of the Landrover were some ropes and some girlie magazines.

'Are you sure you've not seen another cyclist?' said the Welshman.

'Listen. I'm badly lost.'

'Not to worry we've got a map here somewhere.' He unfolded an Ordnance Survey map of the Dales. 'Now then, let's see, red lines, what are they, bridleways or trunk roads? Don't suppose you've got any chocolate or anything have you? I'm starving.'

'Could I have a look at that map for a minute? I said, snatching it off him. I studied it and memorised it detail for detail. If I followed the stone wall that ran north on my left I'd come back onto the drovers' road in about half a mile.

''Bout time we went home for lunch,' said the driver and fired his engine. The radio came on playing a Rod Stewart song from 1975. 'And if you see that scout on a bicycle, tell him he's a tit, right.' And they drove off into the mist.

I felt a strange comfort knowing there was another cyclist out there somewhere. I wished we would bump into each other, if only for moral support. We could weather out the storm together. We could shelter under my cape. He could teach me how to tie bowline hitches and I could teach him the Norwegian for Bob-a-job week. We'd become penfriends and would exchange Christmas cards. We'd be bonded together in the knowledge that we helped save each other's life one August afternoon in the Yorkshire Dales. And, apart from all that, if the worst came to the worst and the weather didn't improve I could always eat him.

I found the drovers' road once more but then inexplicably lost it again. In the distance I could hear the Landrover chugging over the moor, but I kept well clear. I could get lost without any help from those two. I just continued wheeling my bike over the peat until momentarily the cloud cover broke. Through an eye of blue came a ray of sunlight and there far below in the valley was a cluster of houses, smoke rising from chimneys and the distant rumble of lorries on tarmac. 'I wonder if one day that you'll say that you care, like a puppet on a string ... da da dadadada.'

'Lose weight now. Ask me how!' There was that sticker again. This time in a quarry lorry cab window. I was going to ask the driver, how? but he had such a fine belly on him I thought he might take offence. I hadn't hit it off with lorry drivers on this trip so far.

And besides, looking down at myself, my weight problem was a negative one. I was slowly fading away. I'd never been so thin. Instead of developing me into a hunk, all that this exercise had done was turn me into a ten stone drip. Parts of me I'd never seen before were emerging. I was introduced for the first time to my sternum. If I was going to tackle the

Norwegian fjords I was going to need some meat on me. This weekend, I decided, would be an eating one.

Near the scarred and hideous face of Kilnsey Crag I found a converted barn to dry myself out in. This conversion into bunk rooms was the bright idea of a farming couple, and yet the venture hadn't been as successful as they'd hoped.

'Everyone's gone abroad,' said the farmer's wife. 'I was in the travel agents' in Skipton the other day and they were practically giving holidays away. Even the Catteralls from Arncliffe Farm have gone. Greek islands, I think. If you booked up for two weeks you got a free bottle of wine. Demestica, I think.'

Next morning I was up for the six o'clock news. According to my original calculations today was the day I was to cross the Arctic Circle and so I was going to need an early start. At 7.00 the sky was a blue and white mass. By 7.02 it was in turmoil, a cauldron of driven, waterladen cloud. I sat and watched it pour for an hour then hitch-hiked into Gargave to the sheep dog trials.

A sheep farmer picked me up. He was on his way to the trials himself. He even had his dog in the back, an animal with the worst breath I'd ever smelt.

'Is he a sheep dog?' I asked the farmer.

'Who, Jake? Yeah, he's a sheep dog. He's no showman though. He's really stupid.' He turned to the dog. 'Really stupid aren't you, eh Jake? Daft as a brush, right?' On the back seat Jake perked up: 'Who said that? Is someone speaking to me?'

'He's short sighted as well,' said the farmer. 'He never wins a thing. I only enter him so we get in free. The trouble with show dogs is that they're good for showing and nothing else. You can't work them on a farm. They'll only bring back three sheep at a time, like they have to in the trials, and then they expect a trophy and a round of applause and the rest of the day off.'

A sheep dog trial is a cleverly devised test divided into and scored on five stages. The first is the Outrun where the shepherd sends his dog from heel out to the sheep, normally a distance of about three hundred yards. The dog should take a wide Outrun and receive no command until he reaches the sheep, the idea being that the animals aren't disturbed until the dog gets behind them and comes in for the second phase of the operation, the Lift.

The Lift is the collection of the sheep, and is followed by the Fetch, as the dog is instructed to bring the sheep back in a straight line to the shepherd, negotiating an open gate on the way and positioning them for the Drive.

The Drive is the most skilful manoeuvre, requiring the dog to drive the sheep away from the base and through another obstacle, contrary to the dog's natural instinct to drive towards the shepherd. After the Drive comes the Crossdrive across the field and then finally the approach to the pen. Only when all the sheep have been penned can the gate be closed and the exercise concluded.

The Shepherd and Jake and I piled out of the car. The shepherd went to talk to his colleagues. Jake went to talk to his. I followed Jake.

'Oh oh, here comes our Jake, Mr Myopic himself,' said a wasp-waisted collie with a white patch on his eye, Jake was trotting towards him.

'Watch out for't tree Jake. No Jake, we're over 'ere. No, no lad, that's a Cortina. We're over here. That's it.'

'How do Jake.'

'How do Patch, Bing.'

'How do Jake. God! your breath smells. What you been eating?'

'Spar Own Brand dog meat. Who's in't lead then?'

'Margie from Buckden farm.'

'Aye, Margie, mind you she bribed the judge, in't that so Bing?'

'Aye, she went round the back of the horticultural tent with his spaniel.'

'Well I'll go to Fleetwood on a tram'

'We're thinking of putting in an official complaint. It's the fourth time this season. Hang about, here comes Metcalfe.'

Metcalfe came in panting from his run.

'How do, Metcalfe.'

'How do, Jake. God your breath don't half honk. What you been eating? Spar Own Brand?'

'Aye.'

"What are the sheep doing today, Metcalfe?'

'Bright bunch of bastards. Everything were going a treat. I did a good outrun, lifted 'em nice and easy and was going for the fetch when one of the little buggers stops dead in its tracks, looks me in the eye and says: "I put it to you there is no difference between dialectical materialism and existentialism?"'

'No? Would you credit it? What did you do, Metcalfe?'

'I bit it.'

'Good thinking.'

'Who's in't front anyway?'

'Margie from Buckden Farm.'

'Tch! That bitch is going to sleep her way t'Crufts she is ...'

'Shh. Here she comes now. How do, Margie.'

'How do boys. God your breath stinks, Jake. What you been eating?'

'Spar Own Brand.'

'Well it smells like dung. I'm going to the beer tent to see what I can pick up.'

'Aye, we know.'

'Honestly, I don't know what they see in her. I've seen better looking muck spreaders.'

'Hey up, whose whistle was that? Jake. It's yours.'

'Oh aye, so it is. Right, see you lads; wish me luck.'

'Jake! Watch out. Mind that tree ... ooh! Ooh dear!'

Jake bounced off the oak tree and set off up the field. But the problems with being a shortsighted sheep dog aren't easily overcome, the biggest being that you can't see the sheep until you trip over them. Jake's outrun was good insofar as it was fast but it lost him points because when he reached the sheep, instead of circling them he just kept on going. It was only the hamburger van that stopped him. Undeterred he came in for the Lift and the sheep scattered like rice. The rest of the trial was a bizarre farce with Jake sitting in the middle of the field scratching his head and the shepherd going blue from whistling and finally resorting to commands like: 'They're behind you, you stupid dodo!' In the end Jake managed to get himself stuck in the pen and the sheep grazing on the A65 halfway to Giggleswick. He came last. 'Mind you, it was an improvement on last year' said the shepherd as we drove home.

Back at the barn, a young Dutch couple had arrived. They were on vintage mopeds so lacking in power they had to push them up hills. But they'd come a long way, from East Anglia over to Wales and now they were heading up into the North York Moors. The girl took one look at me and said: 'I bought a cape like that. I also went yellow.'

I asked them what they thought of England and they said they preferred Marks and Spencers to C & A. They'd also visited Milton Keynes and Telford:

'Milton Keynes has better ring roads,' said the girl.

'But Telford was more interesting because we couldn't find the middle,' said the boy.

They seemed to have understood England. And they had interesting theories concerning the North and the South:

'The biggest difference,' said the girl, 'is that the people in the South keep gnomes in the gardens, and those in the North keep chickens.' I like the Dutch, I always have.

Two families from Bradford had also arrived. They asked me and the Dutch couple to eat with them. Ten people sitting round a big table in a barn on a starless, wind-driven night in the Yorkshire Dales, drinking plonk and eating second helpings. At the end of the meal the Dutch boy stood up and said: 'Yorkshire people have big warm hearts I think, but an inability to express themselves so they pile food on plates which is appreciated. Thankyou and a very much goodnight.'

He took the words out of my mouth.

Next morning was brilliant, the forecast was good. I packed up my bike, eyeing the sky suspiciously. One of the kids from Bradford was watching me: 'Where are you going?' he asked.

'North. Why, do you want to come with me?'

'Nah. Are you going towards Lake Windermere?'

'Don't think so.'

'Well if you do, see if you can find the kite I lost there last summer.'

'Right.'

I headed off following the River Wharfe. After a few miles I remembered I'd left my cape and hat in the drying room. I thought about going back for them but my cape was a ripped mess and my hat had shrunk, and besides ever since I'd had them it had rained nonstop. Now I'd left them behind the sky was bright blue. I sensed a strange logic there somewhere and I kept on going. If it rained again I'd put my arms through a dustbin liner ('the sensible cyclist always carries a dustbin liner').

I steered a route through the mashed hedgehogs. It was Sunday morning. Strange, there always seemed to be more corpses on the tarmac on a Sunday morning. It must have been because everyone went to the pub the night before. Either the drivers were pissed on their way home or the hedgehogs were.

6. Cumbria: The Power Train

A tearing of alloy. A metallic crack. A sudden loss of resistance from the pedals. The crunch of scrotum on crossbar. The simultaneous ramming of both testicles back up to where they came from.

That's how I always imagined a snapped chain would be. In reality it was rather less painful, just the strange sensation of pedalling like crazy and not going anywhere, followed by the rattle of an oily tail.

But I couldn't have wished for a more beautiful spot to have a breakdown. The River Wharfe babbled next to the road. The smooth fells rose all around me in sunshine and I sat on a grassy bank looking forward to the test of initiative I had been presented with.

One minute later though I was fed up with it. I had problems. I simply didn't have the tools to effect repairs. A chain rivet extractor was what I needed, and on a Sunday morning in the middle of the Yorkshire Dales my chances of coming across one were virtually nil.

'Need a chain rivet extractor?' said a voice from across the road.

I spun round to see another cyclist. A young man with an old bike. He had a thick North American accent and even thicker legs.

'Yes, I'd love a chain rivet extractor, please.'

He plucked one out of his saddle bag and threw it across the road to me and five minutes later my chain was fixed.

His name was Simon and he was a Canadian. He worked in London in oil, but at weekends he strapped his bike to his roof-rack and took off. I said: 'You've saved my life, how can I ever repay you?'

'You could buy me a peach-flavoured yoghurt in the next village,' he said, which seemed like a modest request, and so for the rest of the morning we cycled together.

These dales may have been beautiful, but the gradients were merciless, the steepest I'd come across, we seemed to be forever climbing. And yet cycling with someone made the effort appear minimal. We discussed in depth the wide variety of insects we'd swallowed on our travels. I told Simon what a Red Admiral tasted like and he explained the problems of cycling with spectacles on: 'The flies get caught behind the glass and then bounce back and forward between the lens and the eyeball. It's really weird.'

After the long climb came the long drop. I'd sweated my way up to the top of the pass and taken most of my clothing off in the process, but now freewheeling down, the icy wind whipped up my trouser legs, and my teeth were chattering by the time we arrived in Hawes.

I bought Simon his peach yoghurt, and myself some Wensleydale cheese, and we went to watch the local cricket match.

'I don't understand cricket,' said Simon.

'It's easy,' I said, 'there are two sides. They take it in turns to bat and bowl, and the side that scores most runs wins. Simple.'

We got talking to the man sitting next to us. He said he used to play for Hawes twenty years ago. Now his boy had taken his place whilst he'd become the team's most loyal spectator. They'd had quite a good season because so many

games had been rained off that the team hadn't lost as often
as it normally did.

A Hawes' bowler tossed one up to the batsman who hit a
dolly straight to a fielder. The fielder dithered and the ball
went through his hands as if they were a paper bag, and then
rolled away. The fielder ran after it, bent to pick it up and
kicked it over the boundary for four.

'I could've caught that,' said Simon.

'A child of five could've caught that,' said I.

'My boy that was,' said Hawes' most loyal supporter.

I was following signposts to Lapland (via Dent) rolling over
superb high moorland, the horizon defined by mountains, the
terrain creased with the ubiquitous dry stone walls. A fleet of
evening cloud sailed across the sun and put a patched pattern
of shadows onto the fells. They looked their wildest and best
in this half-light.

I stayed on a farm that night in Dentdale, not far from
Dent railway station on the Settle-Carlisle line, at 350
metres, the highest station in the country. The farmer let me
sleep in a caravan: 'I'll just move my clobber out,' he said. He
was a caver and his clobber consisted of ropes, ladders, lamps
and lots of mud. On Saturday afternoons whilst most people
were watching Grandstand or doing the shopping he was up
to his waist in running water, wriggling through cracks in
the limestone in some dank subterranean maze. 'It's not a
foolhardy sport really,' he said. 'As long as the safety codes
are followed it's no more dangerous than say, cliff-diving at
Acapulco.'

But this fellow was one of the obsessive sorts, you could
tell. He had eyes like a mole, a shuffle like a hobbit and one
of those ridiculous pot-holers' beards.

'He went to Jamaica earlier in the year,' said his wife.
'Came back with a complexion paler than Dracula's, he did.'

'Good caves in Jamaica,' he said.

She gave me food to cook: 'One potatoe, that's twopence. Two eggs, lets say five pence each. One onion and two tomatoes, call them fourpence.' I told her she was too kind and she said: 'You'll find Northcountry folk are all friendly, not like in the city,' and then she gave me a piece of sponge cake to prove her point.

She was discriminating between country and city folk rather than Northerners and Southerners, but that term Northcountry folk was interesting insomuch as there was no Southern equivalent. People in the South didn't regard themselves as indigenous, they didn't call themselves South-country folk. The North had, there was no doubt about it, a solidarity and a pride that didn't exist in the south, and that was commendable and attractive but it probably did as much as any cultural and economic disparity in driving a wedge between the two regions. Northerners had national pride but only really for the North, and like any underdog, when threatened, they consolidated. So as the South grew richer and more self-assured, the North withdrew and became more and more insular.

But it was wonderfully friendly, that was a fact. And yet, I was still having problems of preconception. Take Northern moors, for instance. Traditionally, the only reason anyone ever went up on a Yorkshire moor was to become the victim of a murder or to commit one. That afternoon, I remember seeing a dirty green van parked in a remote layby. In the back were a load of black plastic bags and in the front a man in a dark hat reading a paperback. As soon as I saw him I was convinced he'd just murdered his wife, cut her up into pieces and put her into the bags, and was now reading a book entitled: *How to Dispose of Dismembered Dead Bodies Without Trace*. I felt a shiver as I cycled past.

Whereas if I'd stopped, the fellow would have undoubtedly said hello, offered me his Thermos, told me he was up there because it was a good place to spot Ring Ouzel, and proceeded to reveal secrets it would take a lifetime to glean from your next door neighbour anywhere in the Home Counties: how large his overdraft was, how he'd once touched Norma Liversedge's knee in the choir loft, and how now he was forty-five he'd come to realise he'd never open the batting for Yorkshire.

I just hoped it would be the same in Lapland. There would of course be the language to cope with there, but I was a lone long distance traveller with a ridiculous destination. I wore bright clothes. I tried to make my whole persona say: 'hey, you can trust me!' And I was of the opinion that basically people are friendly everywhere.

However, Lapland, I was beginning to realise, would push that theory to its limits. This new found infamy the Lapps had had inflicted upon them, had publicised all aspects of their lifestyle and their land, attracting much commentary. And the one part of the Lapp character which everyone who'd ever been there seemed to agree upon, was what a miserable, self-centred and unwelcoming bunch of misanthropes the Lapps instinctively were; the sort who would only speak to strangers if they were caught in a bear trap or stuck down a crevasse, and then only to ask to borrow money. Here are two press cuttings I came across written by travellers to the region:

'We had been trekking for hours when we caught sight of a man approaching in the distance. It took forty minutes for us to come within speaking distance, but instead of a greeting, a nod or a smile, we passed without even establishing eye contact.

'I was amazed, and slightly discomforted. Why had we not spoken to the man? I asked of Kimmo (a guide) "there is nothing to say to him. He came here for privacy."'

'I could see the hut after I'd walked for three hours. I fixed my sight on it. Packed away the map and compass and walked harder. There was smoke coming from the chimney. If it was another climber he'd let me sleep; a Lapp would probably tell me to sleep outside and then charge me in the morning.'

There were also many photographs of Lapland in circulation, and these did more than anything to dispel the image of a fairytale kingdom of icicles and Christmas wrapping. The pictures were of a mountainous but stark and smooth-surfaced landscape. Parts of the Dales I'd just been through had looked similarly bleak but I always knew that I was only ever a few miles from a snug village. The Lapps themselves all had hard, lean faces and wore anoraks and baseball caps and were always pictured crouching over a trussed reindeer, brandishing a meat cleaver.

And another thing. In all the reports and in all the photos, not once did a bicycle feature.

The signs told me I was in Cumbria, but I could tell without their help. Passing slowly through England I had been able to notice the style of each region change. Shop fronts may have the same names on them nationwide but looking above to the first floor of a street you can see how a town retains its individuality and its history. I knew Sedbergh was in Cumbria because every picture I've ever seen of a Cumbrian town has had the same black and white trim on the houses, the same sharpnosed gables, the grey green slate and the pot-bellied, purple grained fells on all sides. It was almost the last week in August and the heather was in full flower, but even the earth was purple in these parts.

The terrain was steep, and the roads followed it religiously, but I was tackling these inclines with a sanguine spirit now. After the way I'd climbed the hills around Hawes the previous day I'd realised I was gaining my fitness and could tackle anything this trip might pit me against. Fjords,

Arctic Circles and the North Capes I could take in my stride.
If only I could find my way over to Scandinavia.

My problem was I had no discipline. I was on holiday and
I was meandering. Any cafe I liked the look of I'd stop off for
a cup of tea and a Jacobs' Club. Every village I passed
through I'd think: I'm unlikely to ever come here again, and
so I'd stop and have a banana. Any one who'd talk to me I'd
try and extract a life story from. Any sporting event I'd sit
down and watch until the final whistle. At any striking view
I'd stop and walk a while, just as I did when I came over the
lip of a hill near Tebay to see a railway line, a motorway and
a river winding through the curves of a splendid valley. The
railway was the Carlisle-Lancaster, the motorway the M6,
the river the Lune. And I was above them all on a thin road,
nothing impairing the fine vista of trains, juggernauts and
white water, and the monster of a black cloud mass rolling
inexorably towards me over the opposite fell. It manoeuvred
itself overhead expertly and then dropped its load with such
ferocity that by the time I could hide myself under a sizeable
tree I was awash.

An hour later I was still there, leaning against the trunk
listening to 'Bend Me Shake Me' by The Amen Corner on
the Radio Furness sixties revival show, a constant regurgita-
tion of ephemera concerning Carnaby St and the Maharishi,
only interrupted by an interview with an overexcited man
from Carlisle who had just won the coveted Birdman '86 title
after an unpowered, unassisted flight of 1.7 seconds.

You get to know a tree when you stand under it for an
hour or two. This one had serrated leaves with little hairy
seed sacks, could have been a sycamore, call it a sycamore
anyway. It was moss covered and had a rotten birds' nest
halfway up. Looked at from an angle of sixty-five degrees
from the M6 side, the branches formed an accurate map of
Papua New Guinea. A notice nailed to the wood said 'No
Canoeing' and at eye level someone had carved the initals

J.F.K. This could have been the work of the xxxvth president of the United States of America but was more likely that of Jim 'Figaro' Knutsford from Penrith.

The sun suddenly burst through. The puddles on the tarmac were brilliant. I pedalled off. Two hundred yards later another downpour, another tree, but, more disconcertingly, another snapped chain link.

This tree was rather similar to the last one except the map drawn by the branches was far more redolent of Corsica and the initials were E.C. which could of course have been the work of seminal guitarist and Rock Legend Eric Clapton but was rather more likely that of Ethel Cludd, launderette supervisor from Kendal. What this tree did have, however, which was lacking under the previous one, was another shelterer, a man with a cap and Wellingtons, and a sandwich in his mouth, corned beef and tomato by the look of it. He eyed my limp chain and said:

'Need a chain rivet extractor?'

'Oh, yes please.'

He went to his bike and threw one over to me and five minutes later the chain was whole again.

'I must get one of these,' I said, handing the tool back to him. He had long arms and hands like shovels, though smooth and white as stone.

And stone was what he was working with. He was repairing a dry stone wall. A section bounding a woodland had collapsed and all over the ground were the guts.

'How much do you manage a day?' I asked.

'About six yards.'

And it suddenly occured to me how I'd taken these walls for granted. There were hundreds of miles of them acting as essential stock barriers and demarcation lines all over the Northcountry. I'd just grown used to having them around all day; they seemed part of the landscape. I'd never given a thought to the effort that must have gone into their construction and maintenance. Southern hedgerows were going to seem twee when I got home.

'A good wall should last hundreds of years,' said the waller. 'The secret is, once you've picked up a stone never put it down again until you've found a home for it.' Then his hands moved instinctively to the pile of rubble at his feet. He rummaged around for a minute like a child with a favourite jigsaw then picked up a rock the size of Gibraltar and went to work. He was still holding it half an hour later with arms like a Gibbon's.

Westmorland no longer has an official status. It was discarded the same way as Flintshire and Rutland when the county boundaries were redefined in 1974. It must come as a shock to wake up one morning to the news that the place you've lived in all your life no longer exists. You must start to doubt bureaucracy, particularly when the bureaucrats can't be bothered to even change the road signs. Appleby in Westmorland was the place I was aiming towards and I was going there mainly because it was such a lovely name and looked so attractive printed in black lettering on old white signposts.

I said as much to the tubby salesman I met in the motorway service station on the M6. He said he'd never given it much thought; he never drove anywhere unless it was on a motorway. The M69 from Coventry to Leicester was his favourite: 'Got a lovely camber, the M69,' he said.

He poured a sachet of Sweet an' Low into his coffee. I said: 'I read the other day that saccharin gives you cancer.'

'That's nothing,' he said. 'I read somewhere you can catch Aids from sucking old bus tickets.'

I offered him a bourbon biscuit but he waved it away. He was on an enforced diet, he said.

'Who's enforced it?'

'The company.'

I said I thought companies liked their salesmen to be tubby and jovial, to promote an association with the good life for their product.

'I sell running shoes,' he said.

He was going to Newcastle and he asked if I wanted a lift: 'Chuck your bike in the back, we'd be there in a couple of hours.' But I turned him down. I'd just seen a road map in the service station and noticed the thin line of Hadrian's Wall strung across the top of the country, and I'd thought: what a fine way to enter Newcastle and complete the English section of the trip.

A couple of hours later I was sheltering in the tourist office in Appleby in Westmorland, wishing I'd gone with him. I asked if there was somewhere nearby I could sleep the night, and the woman said there were hundreds of places and gave me a list, plus a plethora of literature on the area's butterfly farms, model railways, glass blowing exhibitions, local craft fayres, abbey ruins and private collections of traction engines on view. I couldn't think of anything I'd rather have done less. Appleby in Westmorland looked such a pretty town with warm stone buildings and I wanted to sit in a warm room somewhere and have limitless tea and toast and read a book until the rain stopped. Surely this highly trained tourist officer could see that. If she was going to suggest activities I'd have preferred her suggestions to be subjective: 'may I recommend you go down past the castle ruins to the Lamb and Flag, the fine old Eighteenth Century coaching house in Folly Lane, and spend the afternoon drinking Forest Brown Ale until you fall over. Alternatively you could go and buy a sausage roll and some bread and butter pudding from Murray's the bakers and then sit in the bus station and read the graffiti.'

I ended up in the Toby Jug cafe where steam from the kitchen made the windows and walls drip. I had toasted tea cakes and sat and counted the postcards from the Greek

Islands stuck up everywhere. There was Santorini and its volcano, not a cloud in the sky, hadn't been one since March no doubt. There was Rhodes, its harbour wallowing in sun and history, not a ripple on the water. There was Crete and a picture of the Hotel Chania, a nice lump of brilliant white concrete amongst the Minoan backdrop. I rubbed the window. Outside, cars had their headlights on. If I'd headed south I'd have been over the Alps by now, half way down Italy, heading to Brindisi and the ferry down to Piraeus.

'It's no wonder we all go abroad for our holidays, is it?' said the woman at the next table steadily working her way through the sugar lumps. She was looking at an old magazine with a front cover picture of Boris Becker blasting his way to the Wimbledon semi-finals. All the spectators were sleeveless and their hands were shading their eyes from the sun.

Another night, another farmhouse, this time in a village a few miles north of Appleby. It didn't look like a farm, more resembled a seaside retirement bungalow, but in the shed where I put my bike I found a cow so I suppose that qualified the place.

I lay on my bed, reading up on Arctic bears, (how they figure heavily in Lapp mythology and how their feet are a delicacy when pickled). Then I stomped down the stairs to try and attract some attention. But the house was silent. The light in the kitchen was on and I pushed open the door to see a line of herb and spice jars arranged in order of height, and a great expanse of trouser bent over an open oven door: – now I remember, when I'd finished writing the letter to DVLC in Swansea I came out of the living room and was going to check the oven when the telephone went again, and it was the same man wanting to know if I was Timothy Whites, I politely told him I wasn't, then went round the flat pulling all the plugs out and shuting doors and it was when I reached the kitchen that I tripped over the dustbin bag that I'd removed from the rubbish container to take out before I left, and while I was down on the floor I noticed the oven was still on and switched it off. Of course!

'Anywhere I can get something to eat?' I said.

Without turning round the trousers said: 'Try the pub.'

I went to the pub. The landlord said he couldn't do snacks because his wife was away. All he said was: 'I wouldn't half get lonely doing a trip like you're doing. But then I get lonely really easily. Whenever my wife's away I get lonely. She's away now and I'm lonely. I may look as though I'm enjoying myself. I may behave like the life and soul of the party but in fact, inside, in here, I'm lonely. That's why I couldn't go on a trip like you're on. I'd get lonely.'

I opened a local newspaper and tried to change the subject: 'I see councillor Bette Binney has successfully opposed those plans to build two flats on that plot of land in Glebe Close.'

'Loneliest I've ever been, in my whole life, without a doubt, was when I was in the army. Now some people say the army was the best years of their lives, – the community spirit, the cameraderie and all that. Not for me it wasn't. I was lonely.'

Back at the farm things had brightened up. The house glowed with electric light. As I walked in, the farmer's wife made such a fuss of me I thought she'd mistaken me for someone else. She told me to go in and sit down in the living room and watch the Minder repeat while she made some sandwiches. She spoke with a soft melodic Cumbrian accent with Scottish words such as Bonnie slipped in. I'd so enjoyed hearing the accents change as I progressed north and now, near the top of the country, here was the sweetest of them all.

'Nothing has changed round here much,' she said. 'It's different in the Dales and Lakes of course, in the National Park, half the houses there are holiday homes now.'

This was common throughout. When industry left the home and went into the factory all the workers had gone with it. Village life and the villages themselves deteriorated. Houses became derelict until that familiar saviour, tourism, marched in. Then the buildings were restored. The pubs and shops found new business. Tourism had changed the villages irrevocably but it had also revived them. And all the locals well realised the potential.

'The trouble with this village is that it's ugly,' she said. 'That's the trouble with this house as well. We only got our tourist board certificate because I pulled the bed away from the wall. You've got to be able to get out of bed on both sides, see.'

'Why's that?'

'In case of fire,' she said and thought about it for a moment: 'I suppose if one side of the bed catches fire, you've got to be able to get out of the other. That's fair enough. You've got to have a chair in the room as well. But things like putting chairs in the room don't really attract tourists, we find. What we really need is a gimmick. If only we had a ghost, or a priest hole. Or if only Gary Glitter had stayed here with the Glitter Band on one of his national tours. Or Nelson with that ever so nice Lady Hamilton. Or best of all if Mary Queen of Scots had slept here, just once, we'd have been made then. Mrs Hunter from Pennine View tells guests Mary Queen of Scots once slept at her house. In the attic room, she says, but I don't believe her. She hasn't got a plaque on the headboard or anything.'

Next morning at breakfast the family all gathered round the radio for the weather forecast: 'Scattered showers,' said the weatherman, 'winds picking up from the west. Cold for the time of year.'

'That's interesting,' said the farmer's wife.

There was nothing interesting about that. It had been the same forecast everyday for the last week.

'What's interesting about that,' I said.

'It's interesting because it's been the same forecast everyday for the last week.'

'Be lovely over the seaside today,' said the farmer, eyeing the blue sky to the west.

'You want to go to Silloth,' said his wife.

She gave me a map. Silloth was on the Solway Firth at the very start of Hadrian's Wall, quite a distance to the west. But I couldn't resist the idea. With ease I put aside all thoughts of fjords and North Capes for the day and pedalled off towards the coast.

Slowly the blue took up a greater proportion of the sky. A Beatle Nostalgia show on the radio played Good Day Sunshine. The trees were beginning to cast shadows on the road. I was in traffic free, open country. There was a big fell to look at on my left and woods with songbirds on my right. A farmer I passed told me there was hardly a hill between here and Silloth. This was the best cycling of the trip. At eleven thirty-six precisely, the sun burst through and all was right with the world. At eleven thirty-eight my chain snapped once more.

I'd thought I was in wild country on the previous occasions when I'd broken down but compared to where I was now those locations were as busy as Arndale Centres. I couldn't see a house anywhere; not a smashed up phone box by the roadside, or a Ford Sierra in the distance; not one strapping Canadian or dry stone waller in sight. I considered my options. An adage on past travels had always been: 'When in doubt: eat!' So I unzipped a banana, and suddenly in front of me was a house where I'm positive there hadn't been one before. The door opened and out stepped a lad dressed in tight black cycling shorts, a skull cap from team Martini, cycling shoes and a tight, bright yellow jersey with the word Campagnolo written all over it. He was pushing a shiny racing bike.

'Got a spot of trouble,' I said, 'wondered if you had a . . . ?'
'Chain rivet extractor? Sure.'

I really *must* get one of these I said to myself again as with
a couple of quick twists the broken link was removed and the
chain rejoined. The problem was, buying a rivet extractor
never occurred to me until the chain broke, and then there
was always somebody handy to lend me their's, so why
bother? But I couldn't go on removing links like this. The
chain would soon be the size of a bracelet. I was beginning to
have trouble finding all my gears. The bike was becoming
pinched, its lips pursed.

'The Reverend John Toft Wesleyan minister died here.
November 19th 1911, after preaching in Heston Newmarket
and Caldbeck.' So says his memorial stone stuck in the verge
just past Caldeck, on the top of a hill as the way ahead
suddenly fills with sky and there in the distance is the first
sight of the Solway Firth. A spectacular panorama, the
Pennines behind, the Cumbrian Mountains to the south, and
ahead across the water the first peaks of Scotland. There are
many far less attractive spots to pass away.

I was enjoying this excursion to Silloth. There were all
sorts of interesting towns and villages to distract me.
Wigton, for example, was of note because unlike every other
town I'd come across it didn't have a surplus of shoe shops in
the shopping centre. A wily entrepreneur had, however,
seen this gap in the market, and added Wigton to the round
of his mobile shoe shop – a lorry with a collapsable side
which he lowered to reveal a fine selection of pink fluffy
slippers and assorted seasonal footwear. I said to him:
'You're the first mobile shoe salesman I've ever come across,'
which seemed to embarrass him a bit.

But when I reached Silloth it was a disappointment.
Everyone had told me how pleasant it was, how the air was
fresh, and how the town was relaxing and pretty, but it was

nothing of the sort, although my first impressions of the place weren't helped by the rainstorm that drenched me as soon as I arrived, and by the now familiar sound of my chain snapping. I sheltered near some beach huts, at the back of a grimy stretch of sand full of weed and jetsam. There were some nice dunes here but the beach didn't look as though anyone had been on it all summer.

A woman with a bicycle came and sheltered in the next hut. I said to her: 'I've been told there's some nice scenery around here.'

'If you want nice scenery stand at the water's edge and gaze across to Scotland,' she said.

I tried, but the Scottish coast was obscured by cloud. It was a fine exhibition of weather though, with sunbeams bursting through intermittently and spotlighting the wind-driven squalls as they rolled in like swarms from the Irish Sea. There should have been a rainbow, but I couldn't see one.

Strangely, the woman in the next hut hadn't offered to lend me her chain rivet extractor, so I said: 'S'cuse me could I borrow your chain rivet extractor?'

'3/16s or 5/8s?' she said.

'Er ... dunno.'

She looked at my sorry chain. 'That's 3/16s. Can't help you, I'm afraid.'

What! This was unheard of. I wandered into town and asked a couple of other citizens of Silloth for help, but they all shook their heads sadly. In the end I decided to stay the night. I'd promised myself I was going to camp out in my bivibag for the first time but the digs I found was so cheap it seemed pointless to. The woman said she didn't normally put people up but if I didn't mind the mess I could stay, and then she turfed her eight year old daughter out of her bedroom and gave the room to me.

'I wonder if you've got a chain rivet extractor I could borrow?' I said

'No, I'm new here,' she replied, then gave me a front door key and that was the last I saw of her.

She certainly was new there. The crotcheted ballerina cover on the toilet roll in the bathroom was the only hint that the house was a lodgings, elsewhere it looked like a building site, and my room like a set from Playschool. There was a child's stool and desk. Crayons and Ladybird books littered the floor and the wallpaper was Humpty Dumpty pattern. I read *The Ladybird Book of the Weather* which confirmed what I had already feared to be true: it rains more in England than in Italy. Then I squeezed myself into the chair and sat at the desk writing Old lakeland Dialect Souvenir Postcards:

Dear Nurse Grimes,

T'oald Ashness Brig is yan o' t'best vews aroond Leakkland, nobbut a couple o'miles or se fray Kezzick, thoo gans alang t'laal lonin ta Watendlath ta git theear. P.S. I think I left your grill on.

Which roughly translated means Ashness Bridge is a nice place and it's near Keswick. P.S. I think I left your grill on.

It was the week prior to Silloth Carnival. Red, white and blue was the theme, which was fortunate since it meant that the shops could just leave up their bunting from the Royal Wedding. In the office of the community news sheet though, the annual celebration was taken rather more seriously. The window was plastered with red white and blue rolls of wallpaper listing Silloth's wealth of attractions: ' ... post office, telephones, betting shops, a golf course, a street cleaner who keeps the streets clean, butchers, taxis, public toilets. The question: what has Silloth got to offer? inspired me to do this window. Who said Silloth had nowt?'

But Silloth looked as though it became a resort because it couldn't think of anything better to do. The docks had declined and it was near the sea, so why not? But now in the peak season it had the abandoned air of a resort in winter. The lone icecream man looked as though he hadn't sold a cornet since the clocks went forward.

I wandered through the town looking for a bike shop I could visit in the morning, but there wasn't one. The cobbled main street was so empty it echoed. There didn't seem to be an electric light anywhere, so why was I thinking of Leicester Square. Presumably because of the starlings. It was the time of evening when they gather in swarms rather than flocks, and sit in trees making a terrible din. A man came out of his house and hit an infested tree with a stick: 'Go on, get out of it you rum buggers!' he shouted. And the birds rose in a clamour, flew off with a madclap of wings, banked as one, then settled in a tree ten yards nearer his house. 'I can't hear bloody Terry Wogan,' he protested.

The rain came again and I ducked into a pub. A one-legged man sat at the bar discussing his new wheelchair with the barmaid: 'See, most people prefer an electric. Me, I prefer a manual.'

'Why's that?' said the barmaid, totally engrossed.

'Why? Because you've got better control with a manual, better grip on the road as well. I've got strong hands, see. I use them as brakes. I need them as well if I get up too much speed going past the golf course.'

'You save money on batteries as well,' said a second drinker at the bar. A man with a highly original pair of glasses stuck together with elastoplast and wire, and somehow balanced on his nose.

'No, I get batteries and things free.'

'You get batteries free?!'

'Aye. I'm handicapped, see.'

'I'd get an electric if I was you then. You could go into Carlisle for the day and get the health service to fork out. Here, you should get a two seater and take a bird over to Windermere. It'd be like one of them sportscars without a roof. Free batteries. Phew! I had to pay sixty quid for these spectacles.'

'Anyone know where I can get a chain rivet remover?' I said.

They all looked at me, suspiciously. There was a long silence, then the man in the wheelchair said: '3/16ths or 5/8s?'

'3/16ths.'

'Try the King's Head.'

But there wasn't even anyone behind the bar in the King's Head. I sat and waited a while as two girls came in and settled themselves in the corner of the room as far away from me as was possible without sitting in the Gents. They spoke in whispers. I lipread their conversation.

'What's that you've got in your ear Kevin?'

'A small mountain in the Andes. They say Aristotle Onassis is made from the same stuff.'

'I once ate three shovels of Wolverhampton Wanderers without swallowing.'

'Yes I went there and watched the dolphins.'

My lipreading isn't up to much.

But in another place where I went to get some supper I met a nice barmaid. She was reading an epic love story, a visceral tale of torrid passion spread over five generations and three continents. It was about two thousand pages long and she was on page six.

'Reckon you'll get through that tonight?' I asked.

'I've read it before. It's from the library.' She spoke as though it was the only book in the place.

'I could never read a book that long,' I said. 'I'd have forgotten the beginning by the time I reached the end.'

'That's why I'm having to read it again.' She closed the book and said: 'You're from the South aren't you?'

'Yes.'

'You all think we've got a disease up here, don't you?'

This seemed a bit strong.

'You think we're all deformed and that if you come up here you'll get cancer.'

Mmm. I surreptitiously checked the exits.

'Whereas it doesn't worry us. It's only a processing plant after all.'

'What?'

'It's only a processing plant. Sellafield. Anyone would think we lived in a nuclear wasteland up here.'

Of course, Sellafield was just down the coast. It had been closed down temporarily that very morning in fact, after above normal deposits of radioactive waste were found in the Irish Sea. And then there was the effect of Chernobyl on this area, indirect insomuch as for the time being people were reluctant to go anywhere near anything connected with nuclear fuel, particularly for a holiday, but also direct, because the radioactive cloud from the burst reactor had been blown across the Norwegian Sea from Lapland and rained over the Cumbrian Mountains. There were restrictions on lamb as a result, and Lakeland sheep farmers had put in a compensation claim for millions of pounds.

I said: 'You mean, people are staying away from Silloth because of Sellafield?'

'Sure they are. Ten years ago, even three years ago, this town was packed at this time. Now even the Lakes are quiet.'

Then she perked up: 'You should be here next week though. It's carnival. Silloth really throbs during carnival.'

But I couldn't imagine Silloth ever throbbing. The only time it ever achieved any prominence seems to have been during the reign of George V when the king's physicians recommended he go for a period of convalescence to either Silloth or Bognor – rival towns for the best and freshest air in the country. Unfortunately for Silloth the king chose Bognor, and now the highest accolade the town can claim for itself is: the town King George V almost convalesced in.

I had my bike repaired in Carlisle in the end. A vandriver gave me a lift the following morning. The man in the bicycle shop looked at my chain and said: 'That's a disgrace.'

'Yes,' I know.'

'You'll need a new one.'

'Yes, I know.'

'And a new block to fit that.'

'Right.'

'And a new sprocket to fit that.'

'Right.'

'And a new crank to fit that.'

'Right.'

'And a new fly wheel to fit that.'

'Right.'

'And a new ... '

'Right.'

'And a new ... '

'Right.'

He made me feel ashamed. I was the only bit of the bike he didn't replace. And I'd had such an enjoyable morning until then as well, walking and hitchhiking along the Solway Firth. I remember thinking to myself: this is how cycling holidays ought to be, no hills, no rain, no hurry and no cycling. I just followed a bleached road through Bowness-on-Solway and Port Carlisle, both salty communities, full of sky and looking very fresh after the harsh and huddled Pennine equivalents.

On the surface, all these Northern villages seemed no different from villages the country over. There'd be a church and a Church Street, a mill and a Mill Lane. There'd be a green and a lovingly looked after cricket square. There'd be wet pavements and roads lined with stinging nettles, a public convenience built out of local stone, a video shop and a garden centre where you could buy raffle tickets with proceeds going to the church roof restoration or kneeler fund. There'd be a Bed & Breakfast sign and a JCB earthmover widening the road. There'd be a coronation bench and a jubilee tree, a silted up canal and an overgrown railway line, and at least one British Telecom engineer halfway up a telegraph pole repairing the lines.

But what they did have that was different was Northern faces, and there are no faces like Northern ones.

7. Border Country: Wheels and Tyres

Lappish belongs to the Fenno-Ugric group of the Ural-Altaic languages, the others being Syryen, Vogel, Votiak, Finnish, Hungarian, Mordvinian, Cheremessian and, last but not least, that old favourite, Ostiak.

But then there are three different divisions of Lappish, and even those are split into dialects. To begin with I thought I'd be clever and attempt to gain a basis in one of the most common but there are no Lappish grammar books in English, no English-Lappish dictionaries and being so far removed from the main stream of European tongues, the spoken language would have sounded totally alien to me. Almost as alien as that shouted by the Newspaper vendor outside The Lanes, Carlisle's equivalent of the Arndale Centre. I listened to him for a while and concluded he was in fact speaking English, probably a Geordie sub-dialect. The fascinating thing was he managed to make the news sound catastrophic and at the same time not worth bothering about.

In W.H. Smiths and Marks and Spencers there were Back To School advertisements and the city centre was full of kids following each other round the precincts, bored stiff with the holidays. Two approached me as I wondered round the Roman ruins.

'Give us fifty pence and we'll look after your bike.'

'Get lost.'

'Go on, give us fifty pence and we'll make sure it doesn't get nicked.'

'Push off.' Two nine-year-olds running a protection racket.

'Give us some of your nuts and raisins then, and we'll guarantee your tyres don't get slashed.'

'It's a deal.'

I was touchy about my tyres. Although the truth was, I was longing for a puncture. A month into the trip and I still hadn't had one. It was uncanny, as if the rubber had developed some strange vulcanised quality that repelled sharp objects. But all this did was make me become edgy waiting for the first deflation. I was frightened I'd not have one all the way up to the Arctic Circle, and then hear a telltale hiss as I was being chased across the tundra by a bear.

I looked round the Roman remains, forts notably. Hadrian's Wall runs through Carlisle and you can follow its line by walking over the cricket ground (try and do it during the tea interval) and then on through Willowholme Industrial estate (ask permission before walking through the canteen at Bejam.)

I got back to the bike. One of the kids said: 'Give us a banana each and we'll tell you where your pump is.'

Past Carlisle the first road signs for Newcastle appeared, and just seeing the name fired my enthusiasm all over again. I could sense the English section of the journey drawing to a close and a new one beginning. I felt keen and I quickly reached Brampton. Unfortunately, I really liked the place and decided to stay.

The old moot hall was very much the focal point of Brampton, a timbered, circular construction stuck in the middle of the square, surrounded by market stalls. And there in the middle of them, sitting under a mountain of pink fluffy slippers, I noticed my friend the mobile shoe shop salesman.

A surprise really because Brampton had its fair share of footwear outlets. In fact, the most famous building in the town is a shoe shop. According to the plaque on the wall in 1745 it had been Bonnie Prince Charlie's headquarters during the siege of Carlisle.

I said hello to the mobile shoe shop owner and he gave me the kind of smile that said: 'Who the hell are you?' Then he recognised me and said: 'Couldn't think who you were to start with, then I remembered your pullover.'

A pub was offering accommodation and a meal for a bargain price and I checked in. The room was triangular, with windows in the roof and walls. It would have been like a hothouse, but in fact what it meant was the rain came at you from all angles. It was the middle of August and the central heating was on.

I lay on the bed and tuned into Test Match Special. But the match had been rained off. I listened to the Archers instead: Elizabeth had passed one of her A-levels and had decided to leave home and open a boutique. Then the batteries went flat again and so I learnt the Norwegian for 'Thank you it's been a wonderful evening' is '*Tusen takk Det har Vaert en veldig hyggelig kveld*,' and adjourned to the bar.

On the television the Miss U.K. finals were about to begin. Miss Portsmouth swaggered down the catwalk and said, 'I'd like to make a parachute jump and travel.' A young Scottish woman sitting at the bar said: 'I've always wanted to travel. Never been that keen on parachuting, but travel, yes. I've always wanted to go to Egypt. I suppose I'm what you could call an Egyptologist. Unfortunately, I'm frightened of the curse.'

'What curse?' I said.

'The curse. I mean, look at Lord Caernarvon. Discovered the tomb of Tutankhamen and then died under suspicious circumstances, just like all the rest of them.'

'The rest of who?'

'The rest of the people who saw Tutankhamen.'

'I saw Tutankhamen.'

'Well I wouldn't like to be in your shoes.'

A man with a cardigan gone at the elbows, armpits, cuffs, collar and pockets joined us. He was drunk. He screwed his eyes together and tried to focus on me. 'Haven't we met somewhere before?' he said.

'Don't think so.'

'Five years ago in the Seychelles?'

'No I'd have remembered.'

'I looked a lot different then.'

'No, I'd have remembered if I'd been to the Seychelles, I meant.'

'I know. It was in the Royal Oak, Newquay, last summer, August.'

'Nope.'

'Sure I didn't meet you in the Granada service station on the M6 in January? You lent me a windscreen defroster.'

'No, couldn't have been me. I don't have a windscreen defroster.'

'How about in the White Hart in Cardiff?'

'No.'

'I know. You work for Hollings and Barrington in Felixstowe, in their packing department.'

'Nope.'

He was an insurance salesman. He spent his life driving up and down the country.

'I've got a memory for faces,' he said.

'No, you haven't,' said his wife.

'Do I know you?' he said. She was standing there holding his overcoat, trying to get him to come home.

'I know. It was in Wembley Conference Centre, in June. International Insurance Salesmen Convention.'

'Nope.'

His wife was Czechoslovakian: 'I've lived in Prague and in

Munich,' she said, 'and now I live in Brampton.' When she thought of her first two homes, her eyes looked brightly into the past. When she thought of Brampton they swerved to the corner of her face and were thrown into her head along with her glass of whisky.

'I know, I know,' said her husband, prodding me, 'the Rose and Crown, right, am I right?'

'That's this pub, darling,' said his wife and dragged him towards the door.

'See, I knew I'd seen him before.' He put his hat on. Then as he left: 'I reckon you'll be all right with that Scottish bird, the Egyptologist. She fancies you.'

I smiled at her. She smiled back. Behind her Miss Rochdale strode up the catwalk, swivelled once, said her ambition was to be a dental receptionist and then made an exit stage left.

But I had plans for the evening. It was festival week in Brampton and the Brampton players were presenting, for two nights only, Festival Variety and I was the lucky holder of a first night ticket.

The show was to be staged in the Brampton Playhouse, a converted chapel, held up by scaffolding provided by Carlisle Scaffolding Ltd Tel. 48484. Inside was a great crack all the way down one wall provided by Carlisle Cracks in Walls Ltd. Tel 84848. I bought a programme and the compulsory raffle ticket then found a seat as near to the guest of honour, the deputy mayor, as I could. As I sat there I thought back over the vast assortment of raffles I'd supported over the summer. Raffles for church roofs, old folks minibuses, playschools, and countless other doubtlessly worthy causes. If I'd won all the prizes, I'd now be travelling with a fridge freezer, a bottle of sherry, a side of beef, a lawn mower, a set of patio furniture, an electric blanket, a food processor, fitted sheets, a fruit cake and innumerable cuddly toys strapped to my bike. As it was I'd won nothing. Now in Brampton I was in the running for a box of Roses chocolates, proceeds going towards repairs to the Playhouse. The draw was to be made at the interval by the fourteen-year-old carnival queen sitting in the front row, heavily chaperoned, and if I didn't win I was going to get stroppy.

There was an audience of about a hundred, which made the large room look empty and feel cold. Overcoats were kept on. Outside, the traffic thundered past along the wet A69. Finally, a man in a dinner jacket came on and confirmed what was already written in the programme: 'Patrons are reminded that due to circumstances beyond our control the Brampton Players have had only some two weeks' rehearsal for this show and therefore ... ' Before he could finish a heavy bass line jumped out of the speakers and a disco beat filled the hall. The lights on the stage began to flash, the curtains were pulled back (well, one of them was,) and there was Pamela Murphy and her disco dancers getting the show underway, gyrating to a medley of hits from the sixties. You could guess which was Pamela Murphy, she was the only one with a developed chest, the only one who knew the steps and the only one to stop dancing at the same time as the music. Back came the M C and launched himself into an energetic recital of a Stanley Holloway monologue. But again he was interrupted. This time for: 'The owner of a Ford Sierra C869 VHY to remove his vehicle from the A69 or the police will prosecute, thank you.'

A vocalist took over, singing songs from the South West. He had all the lighting, a slick outfit and a stylish pianist with a synthesizer, but he was hindered by his inability to remember the words or the tune of the song. He was followed by a collection of Irish folk singers, some highland dancing and some more songs from the South West which the audience were very appreciative of and didn't laugh when the scenery collapsed or the performers tripped up. Pamela Murphy and her dancers returned to do more hits from the sixties, although their carefully choreographed interpretation of Puppet on a String was rather spoilt by the arrival of a bagpipes player in the last verse.

The finale arrived. The cast did everything they could to get the audience to join in the singing, and then as soon as we did they did everything they could to get us to shut up again. There were no encores. The curtain fell. The raffle was drawn. I won nothing. I didn't get stroppy. As the audience filed out someone said: 'I hear the Worksop lass won Miss U.K.'

The festival was continuing but I decided to give the Brampton and District Silver Band and Bowling Club bazaar and the Festival It's A Knockout a miss and spend the next day along Hadrian's Wall. I didn't even intend to go to the coffee morning in aid of the church restoration fund held in the moot hall, but I got so drenched trying to cross the market square that halfway over I decided to take shelter.

'My God! How far have you come?' said the woman in charge who I recognised as one of the Brampton Players. She sat me down and poured me out a coffee.

I confessed I'd only come from the other side of the square and she said: 'oh,' and then shoved a collection tin under my nose. 'The church needs £6,000 to survive.'

I reduced the amount to £5,999.70 and she said, 'The problem at the moment is that we haven't got a vicar.' She spoke as though they were a struggling football team without a manager.

I bought a couple of raffle tickets for a tin of Peak Freans Assorted and set off in a break in the rain. I got as far as the A69 before I had to take shelter again, this time in a dome-like summer house on a green with trucks hurtling past me. It's said that the Lapps suffer psychologically from the long periods of darkness during the winter months. Depression is commonplace and there is evidence to link the high Scandinavian suicide rate with the seasonal lack of sunlight.

I was beginning to wonder if rain might ever effect the folk of North West England similarly. This morning in the moot hall they'd all laughed about the frost the previous evening and made jokes about the rain, how it was only raining in between showers, and how it had only rained once this week – from Monday through to Friday. Their good humour managed to keep their spirits up, but the strain was beginning to show:

'This rain's ruined my dahlias,' said a man who had joined me in the shelter, 'it breaks my heart, it does,' and he stamped his foot in irritation. In Hammerfest he'd have put a gun to his head.

Eventually, I reached Gilsland, where the visible remains of Hadrian's Wall begin. The scenery took over here and the rain didn't matter anymore. Ahead was the Whin Sill, the feature of the landscape that was with me all day, a series of waves of rock and crag, with a sheer drop on the north side, the perfect site to establish a defensive line.

Somewhere along the way I'd picked up a tourist board question and answer leaflet concerning the Wall, a succinctly written document which managed to compress four centuries of Roman rule into a side of A4:

Q. What is Hadrians's wall?

A. A fortification to mark the northern frontier of the Roman Empire. Created by the Emperor Hadrian in about 122 AD, its job was to keep at bay the barbarians from the north.

Q. How long was it in use?

A. From 122 AD to about 400 AD.

Q. What sort of fortification was it?

A. A complex of ditch, wall, road, rear earthwork and a series of forts, fortlets and turrets.

Q. What size was the wall?

A. 15 feet high, 10 feet wide and 73 miles long, stretching from the Solway to the Tyne.

Q. What is a milecastle?

A. A fortlet built onto the wall every Roman mile (slightly less than a modern mile).

Q. How much of the wall is left?

A. Not much.

But of what was left the best preserved parts were east from Gilsland, and I decided to dump the bike and walk along the Pennine Way which emerged here once more. The views of the Wall were superb now as it rose and dipped and snaked away into the distance along the contour of the sill. In some places it was a well reconstructed and solid fortification, in others a lowslung affair, thrown together from surrounding rubble and not so much Hadrian's Wall as Farmer Geordie's stock barrier. There was an enormous sense of history to be felt all along its length but once again it was the raw material that was most impressive. The Wall was a monument to Northern stone, the ubiquitous grey that was always just breaking the surface; the underlying colour of the North. It was in the earth, in the sky, and in the people's skin.

I reached the remains of a fort and climbed to the top and looking to the north was like gazing out to sea. I was standing on a cliff. The land beyond was on a lower level and I could see to the horizon as the terrain rolled bleakly away. A bright red GPO van followed a thin black road towards the horizon. It went over a cattle grid and there was a time lapse before you heard the rattle. The land looked so wild and untouched but it was all National Park, all managed, grazed or hill farmed. It should have been wilderness, but there was no such land left in England. Even the mountains were grazed. The last English wolf was killed in 1749.

The peace was broken by a sudden blast of jet engines and for the rest of the morning fighter planes performed aerobatics overhead, running through their low level flying manoeuvres. Like almost every other designated Area of

Outstanding Natural Beauty in this nation, the environs of Hadrian's Wall have an MoD presence, in this case the rocket monitoring station at Spadeadam. Every so often the pilots are let out with their expensive toys and they hop over the hedgerows twisting and turning, doing somersaults and playing chicken. The sheep and the birds seemed used to it all, but it terrified me. At one point a plane came so close I could count the rivets on its belly and when it disappeared over the Wall such a noise rent the air I was convinced the thing had crashed and I ran up the hill expecting to see a heap of smoking metal. But there it was, already about three miles in the distance, pulling itself straight up into the sky like a missile.

I walked back to my bike. Unfortunately, it hadn't been stolen so I continued into Hexham, the drizzle wetting me, the wind drying me. Corn on the cob were on sale in Hexham market, so were marrows. The summer was on a downward slope. I cycled over the Tyne out of town. And now I was no longer avoiding fragments of shattered windscreen and broken bricks lying in the road. If I didn't have a puncture soon I was going to scream.

When you're cycling to Lapland and you're planning on taking the boat from Newcastle, and you set out from Hertfordshire and you suddenly find yourself in Scotland, then you know things are going seriously wrong.

I wasn't quite sure how I'd got there. Everyone seemed to be heading north to Edinburgh, a procession of vintage cars, motorcycle combinations, hitchhikers and people pushing prams for charity. I was led astray by the festival spirit and by the weatherman who'd said: 'There's a distinct possibility that there might be a sunny interval today, although I'm not promising anything.' So I had my shorts on and I was cycling for the fun of it towards the border and Kielder Water, the largest man-made lake in Europe.

'That's as maybe,' said the old man in Falstone where I stopped to watch a display of traction engines, 'but it hasn't half mucked up the fishing round here.' He was tinkering with a peculiar looking machine consisting of a tangle of pipes, pistons and cylinders. Suddenly it burst into life and began sucking up water from one bowl, pumping it through a tube and depositing it in another. A complete and utter waste of energy.

'Mucked up the weather as well, that dam has,' he said. The rumour was that since the valley had been flooded the weather pattern had been irrevocably altered.

'It's all this photosynthesis business,' he went on. 'The summers were a lot warmer and sunnier when I was a lad. I've got two pullovers on today. We're in a corridor of climatic change round here. I read that in a magazine.'

There'd been a lot written about Kielder Water in magazines. The original scheme was a dynamic one, drawn up after much deliberation and research into the projected water needs of the Tyne and Wear district. The forecast was that the present water supply would be unable to cope with the area's industrial needs by the end of the century, not because the rivers couldn't supply the water, but because the flow couldn't be regulated to feed industry at a constant rate all year round. Some sort of networked scheme was needed and so the plan was proposed to flood the Kielder valley, dam it at Falstone and regulate the supply to all the North East. Pumping stations downstream on the Tyne would feed the Rivers Wear and Tees, and thus a regional water grid would be created.

Nice idea. Kielder was destined to be the reservoir system that saved the North East and projected it into the 21st century. But hardly had work on the scheme begun than it became clear Tyneside industry was going to suffer at the hands of the recession far beyond the level forecast. The proposed industrial development was cut ruthlessly as steelyards, shipyards and mines closed. Water demands were suddenly drastically reduced, and all the while the level at Kielder was slowly rising.

But rather than abandon the project, the water board pressed on, finishing it in style in 1982 with an inauguration by the Queen. Then they turned it into a windsurfing club.

I cycled slowly around the shores. As far as the eye could see was water backed by forestry plantation. It was a man-made landscape, and I was thinking how drowned valleys could get monotonous after a while when my attention was caught by the couple riding a tandem ahead of me. If, as I'd read on car rear windows, Young Farmers do it in wellies, and windsurfers do it standing up, then cyclists do it ever so quietly, and I heard their conversation long before I reached them.

'I know, you be Sarah Ferguson and I'll be Prince Andrew.'

'No, you be an international investment broker and I'll be an air hostess on Concorde.'

'No, we did that last week. I know, you be Selina Scott and I'll be the gasman come to read the meter.'

'No, you be a lifeboatman and I'll be a dinghy sailor in distress.'

Actually, that was one of the more interesting cycling conversations I'd heard. They were normally far more mundane. Cyclists felt obliged to acknowledge each other as they passed, which showed a certain solidarity, but few seemed keen to stop. It was normally a case of:

'Hellooooo ... '

'Hellooooo ... '

And you were already a hundred yards apart.

As I crossed the border into Scotland however, I saw a cyclist by the side of the road, bike upturned and a wheel off. I pulled over: 'How do,' I said.

'Sod off.' He was Scottish and in a temper.

'Want to borrow a chain rivet extractor?' I said – I'd splashed out on one in Carlisle.

'What do I want a bloody chain rivet extractor for, oaf? I've got a puncture.'

God, I'd love a puncture, I thought.

'This is my tenth puncture this trip, this is,' he said. 'I wouldn't mind but I've only been going two days. I had a puncture in Duddingston, Dalkieth, Dunbar, Duns, Dundock, Dryburgh and Denholm. You name it and if it begins with a D I've had a puncture there!'

'Dunfermline?'

'Aye.'

'Dundee?'

'Aye.'

Dundalk?'

'Aye.'

'Where're you heading?'

'Well, I was going to Dumfries, but I'm not so keen now. There's the little bugger!' He'd found the hole and patched it then calmed down a little and asked me where I'd come from.

'Hertfordshire.'

'How many punctures?'

'None.'

'None?!!'

'None. I don't know how to get them.'

'You lucky bastard. You lucky, lucky, lucky bastard! Which way did you come?'

'Up through Shropshire, Manchester, Yorkshire, Cumbria.'

'Nowhere beginning with D?'

'Er ... '

'You lucky bastard. You lucky, lucky, lucky bastard! I hope you fall off.'

A good job I didn't tell him about Derbyshire.

The regimentation of Kielder's incipient forests passed and I entered the beautiful Border Country. Now there were thistles everywhere, and there on the road ahead of me was an addition to my wildlife log. A rat, the first of the trip. Neatly squashed, not messy at all. It's tail laid out straight behind it. Morris Marina job by the look of it.

Just past it I saw a broken bottle in the road. I swerved and rode straight over it. My tyres didn't flinch.

It was almost dark when I reached Jedburgh. The new football season had begun that afternoon and Celtic fans dressed in green and white hoops were parading up and down the main street. I asked a couple if Celtic had won but they weren't sure: 'It was either Celtic or the other lot.' They were drunk, the whole town looked drunk. I'd planned to sleep out that night but another frost was due, said the weatherman, so I found a B&B above a butcher's. As I arrived the young landlady was laying the table for breakfast.

'I always lay the table on a Saturday before I go out. I'm too pissed to when I come back. I like to enjoy my Saturday nights.'

I like to enjoy my Saturday nights as well and I asked if I could join her. She led me down a back street, quiet to look at, just a line of closed shops, but there at the end was one building bulging at the seams, straining to break loose from its foundations. Each time the door opened a blast of music and smoke escaped into the street.

A thin line of people filed inside to a bar where everyone stood to attention, not out of choice but because there was no room to relax a limb. In the corner a television played a video of King Kong. The bi-planes were buzzing round the Empire State Building. King Kong clung to the spire swatting them with Fay Wray in his fist. He began to totter. The music stopped. As his grip on the building loosened the entire pub turned and watched in silence as the much misunderstood monster fell to the streets. There was a crash and a cloud of dust, and then everyone resumed their conversations.

When I got back to my landlady with drinks she'd been cornered by the rugby team. One of them said to me: 'you don't want to take any notice of those football supporters out there, this is a rugby playing town,' as if that gave the team the right to grope any woman in the place. But my landlady didn't seem to mind. She'd said she like to enjoy her Saturday nights. I lost her in the milieu and somehow or other gained the undivided attention of a heavily intoxicated sailor, a man who spoke in an accent that sounded very similar to Norwegian. I experimented with a few phrases from the At The Singles Bar section of my phrase book:

'*Er de ledig i kveld?*'

(Are you free this evening?)

He looked at me suspiciously, swayed a little and pushed his face up to mine and said, 'Ssh, dinny tel noon.'

'*Kunne de tenke Dem a ga ut og danse?*'

(Would you like to go dancing?)

'Scrun de noon do heavie.'

'I see. *Skal vi go pa kino?*'

(Shall we go to the cinema?)

'Nots the veri, sonny,' he said and put his glass down on the counter.

'*Kan jeg skaffe Dem en drink?*'

(Can I get you a drink?)

'I'll have a pint of heavy please, that's very kind of you.'

I bought him a pint of Heavy and he insisted I have one. It filled me full of air and made me feel dizzy immediately.

'*Tusen takk. Det har vaert en veldig hyggelig kveld. Kan jeg fa treffe Dem i morgen,*' I said.

(Thankyou for a lovely evening. Can I see you tomorrow?)

'Stren dol extrum ssh do noon.'

I felt cold and ill, and I went home and slouched on the couch in front of the television, assuaged by a cup of tea and the finest sight of any summer: David Gower stroking a Test Match century.

Sunday 24 August was notable for two announcements. The first by doctors who claimed that drinking hot liquids or eating hot foods too quickly could cause cancer. The second by Mr Foggitt, the 73-year-old weather sage from Thirsk in Yorkshire, who admitted he based his predictions on the behaviour of the moles in his garden. The year had started well for Mr Foggitt when he correctly predicted a warm spell for Wimbledon in mid-June, but his mistake was to insist that once here the warm spell would last for the rest of the summer. 'The moles were going crazy,' he said in his own defense, 'running round the place. Nothing but activity. It had to be a sign of warm weather. Maybe they were just having a joke at my expense. Moles are like that.'

I was following the base of the Cheviots, heading east now through more of this glorious Border Country. In the distance smoothsided peaks rose like a line of bald heads, and the vegetation was so lush. There were fruit farms here again, more PYOs. The verges were thick and wet. There were hedgerows and the fields were all activity as the hay was harvested.

Only in one department did the Border Country lose marks. The standard of scarecrows was appalling. Nothing was going to be frightened by these limp arrangements of plastic bags and string slung over a stick and stuck in the field like a bean pole. Even sparrows walked up to them and stuck their tongues out. I'm sure scarecrows were a lot scarier in the days when the summers were a lot warmer.

I was daydreaming, imagining what a scarecrow would look like if Gerald Scarfe designed it, and I didn't hear the Midlands Tandem Association annual tour '86 aproach me from the rear. I just felt a sudden intake of air, a blast of hot breath on the back of my neck, and ten cyclists swept past on five bikes, chrome sparkling, moving parts glistening with 3 in 1. Twenty muscular legs powering the machines smoothly forward, luggage on the back, glucose bottles strapped to the frame, maps folded in dinky perspex holders over the handlebars.

I followed them into Kirk Yetholm where we all stopped at the pub. I said hello but all I got was a nod. These were serious cyclists, flatcapped and skintight, not only had they shaved their legs, I was sure I'd caught a whiff of Old Spice as they passed. They took one look at the state of my Arctic Circle Tourer and I was ostracised.

The pub in Kirk Yetholm marks the end of the Pennine Way. Anyone who has walked the path in its entirety can proudly enter the bar and order a half pint of beer and put it on the slate of that doyen of the hiking fraternity Alfred Wainwright. It would seem easy to take advantage of such a gesture, but ramblers aren't that sort of people, and anyway it's easy to tell those who have just finished the path from those who have just returned from a morning's stroll. The latter have glowing complexions and they sit and swop rambling anecdotes in a civilised manner. They laugh occasionally. The former sit covered in dung. They have bags under their eyes, grey skin and they communicate with the kind of noises you'd expect from people who have had nothing but sheep for company for the previous two or three weeks.

A couple of lads sat on the terrace. They'd just walked the two hundred and seventy miles and now they swigged down their free half pint and about six more behind it. I was lying flat on a bench when one of them nudged me.

'How do,' he said.

'How do.'

'Been walking the path I have, the Pennine Way.'

'Have you?'

'Aye. The Pennine Way from start to finish. You bet we have. Here Dave, he says, have we been walking the path? You bet we have. We started out two weeks ago and we haven't seen nowt but peat bogs and sheep since. It's a tough trek, I tell you. Right tough. You cycling are you?'

'Yes, I'm cycling to ... '

'Honestly, there were times when I thought we'd never get beyond the next wall. Times when I thought we'd never see Hull again. In't that right Dave? Cycling a long way are you?'

'Well, yes I ... '

'You wouldn't believe some of the hills we've climbed. Absolutely sheer. You spend all morning looking at the sky and all afternoon looking at your feet. Dave was up to his neck in mud once, weren't you Dave? Funny moment that was. In fact it was the only funny moment, and Dave didn't find it altogether hilarious. Dave often thought he'd never see Hull again as well, and him with his ingrowing toenails. Nice cycling weather this in't it?'

'Not bad, been a bit ... '

'We had some weather I can tell you. Did we have some weather or what. You see most people think the Pennine Way is a doddle. They think anyone can put a rucksack on their back and potter off with a couple of meat pies and an Esso leisure map and they'll be all right. But it's not like that; you can't underestimate the Pennine Way. Dave underestimated it the day he fell into the mud and he's got geology O-level haven't you Dave? or is it history? Anyway. Get some pints in Dave there's a good lad. So, where have you cycled from?'

'St. Alb ... '

'My goodness, look at those tandems.'

The walker went over to The Midland Tandem Association annual tour '86.

'Are you cycling?' he asked one of the women.
'Yes,' she said.'
'Where from?'
'Well, we started out in ... '
'Just walked the Pennine Way we have, me and Dave.
Bloody tough I tell yer. Many times I thought I'd never see
Hull again. Got through forty-six elastoplasts in two weeks
I did, ain't that right Dave?'

I rode out of Kirk Yetholm and over the bridge back into
England, and suddenly it was Bank Holiday. I had an ice
cream, visited a craft fayre, generally tried to get myself into
the swing of things, but there was something decidedly
unbank holidayish about that afternoon. And it was as I sat
watching a cricket game in conditions ruined by the ever
more forceful and icy wind that I began to feel something
unfriendly was brewing. The outfield was strewn with
leaves, and the umpires wore overcoats as from one end a fast
bowler had difficulty making the ball travel the statutory
twenty-two yards, while from the other crease a spinner
took wicket after wicket with meteorite off breaks the
batsman never saw. It was a funny game to watch, but
branches were beginning to break off the trees and tiles to
slip off roofs. The tail end of Hurricane Charlie was
preparing to whip across the country and August was about
to get angry.

The boundaries of Lapland today are inexact and reflect
more a change in lifestyle than territory. But demarcation
lines once existed, determined by two familiar criteria: fish
and reindeer. Sweden, Finland, Norway and Russia all
desired access to the fishing grounds off the Arctic Circle,
but the competion was gentlemanly until Charles IX of
Sweden started to get pretentious and gave himself the
inflated title of King of the Lapps in the Land of The North.
The Lapps said 'big deal' and went on fishing and farming

reindeer wherever they wanted. But Charles meant business. He began to build forts on the Finnmark coast and then very magnanimously told the Dutch they were welcome to go fishing off Norway. This sort of behaviour, quite understandably, annoyed his neighbours, particularly King Christian or Norway, who told the Dutch they were just as welcome to go fishing off Sweden. In 1611 Christian declared war on Charles. Not to be outdone Charles immediately declared war on Christian. Christian's response was to declare another war on Charles, which provoked a similar reaction from Charles. Eventually, in 1613 Christian announced he had won the war, which was a coincidence because in the same year Charles made an identical claim. The outcome of all this was a revised delineation of Northern Scandinavia, to which once again the Lapps said 'big deal' and carried on fishing and farming reindeer wherever they wanted.

In this respect Lapland has a lot in common with Berwick upon Tweed, the town on the Scottish-English Border which must suffer from a severe identity problem. It's so obviously Scottish in style and heart, and the river it lies on the north bank of, the Tweed, is such a natural frontier, it seems ridiculous that Berwick should be sited on English soil, an anomaly that has annoyed the Scottish, to whom it originally belonged, throughout history.

Under the Scottish the town flourished. They wanted Berwick as a major port, as a southern link to the continent. England wanted it because Scotland had it. The result was that between the years 1172 and 1482 the town changed hands thirteen times. It seemed whenever the English were bored or they couldn't find a Crusade to occupy their time, the King said: 'I know, let's go and sack Berwick.' As it was, the town became a sort of testing ground for ballistics.

'Got this great new weapon, your Majesty. It's called the long bow.'

'Long bow, eh? I like the sound of that. Go up to Berwick and see if it works.'

And the long bow did work, as the French later discovered at Agincourt.

But, each time the English took Berwick, hardly were their backs turned than the Scots rallied and turfed them out again. The local townsfolk had to look in the final edition of the evening paper each day to see who was in control. The situation was getting silly and eventually in 1482 the town was ceded to England after a long siege and has remainded so ever since.

At least that's what it said in the guide book I found in my guest house on the Newcastle Road. It was one of two books on offer to guests, the other being *The Man from Uncle Book Number 7, The Radioactive Camel Affair* which I'd already read. Outside, the rain was being blown horizontal. Trucks slid down the road to the Tweedmouth Docks, their brakes locked, their windscreen wipers struggling, the drivers peering through the gloom. It was Bank Holiday Monday in Berwick.

So bad was the gale my landlady had told me to keep my bike inside, and so there it stood in the living room between the television and the breakfast table. There'd be no cycling until this blew over. My landlady joined me at the window. She coughed and smoked simultaneously and spoke with an outrageous French accent.

'In France they are having forest fires,' she said.

'In Spain they're sweltering on the beaches.' I said, and then I spent the rest of the morning taking my wheels to bits, testing the spokes, straightening the rims, checking the valves, trying to control a growing urge to stick a pin in a tyre just to relieve the tension.

Berwick's defences, built by Elizabethan military engineers, make it one of the finest examples of a walled town in Europe. It has some splendid bridges as well, three of them:

the imposing 125 foot high Royal Border Bridge built in 1847 for the railway by Robert Stephenson, the Royal Tweed Bridge built in the 1920s to carry the A1 into Scotland, and the low seventeenth-century Jacobean foot bridge, the one I took as I walked into town later that day. Although, crossing it was like trying to walk a tightrope, the wind doing its best to throw pedestrians over the parapets. In the water a hundred swans huddled together under the arches for shelter, and above, seagulls had a battle on their wings just to remain stationary.

And Berwick looks at its best from outside its walls, from the other side of its river. Inside, it has lost most of its old buildings. It's a clutter of one way streets and fish and chip cafes and on that particular afternoon it was empty but for a few trippers looking at displays in the closed shops. Most popular were the travel agents' windows where you could stare at the pictures of sundrenched Ios, and the Rumbelow's window which was showing highlights of the Royal wedding on video. I'd seen it so many times now I knew each camera angle, each wave, by heart:

'No-one puts on a show of pageantry like the British, do they?' I said to the woman in the pac-a-mac next to me.

'You know I think foreigners are just a little bit jealous of our royal family,' she replied.

In the evening, as the town rattled in the wind I sat in a pub where a grandfather clock ticked-tocked each passing second and the barmaid sat in the corner biting her nails. I was the only person in the place and I still couldn't catch her attention. I was beginning to feel my enthusiasm for Lapland drain when a video machine next to me said in a monotone:

'Play me, play me.'

'Pardon?'

'Play me, play me.'

'What do you mean, play me?'

'Insert a coin.'

'Okay,' I inserted a coin. 'There done that.'

'My name is Number Recorder Fortune.'

'Hi. I'm Mark.'

'Win a fortune.'

'Sounds good to me.'

'Play me, play me.'

'All right, all right, don't get impatient. What do I press?'

'Insert a coin.'

'I've already inserted a coin.'

'Win a fortune. Win a fortune.'

'Listen sunbeam, you and I could fall out very quickly.'

'My name is Number Recorder Fortune. Insert a coin.'

'I want my money back. Give me my money back.'

'Play me and win a fortune. Press button to play.'

'Ah, that's more like it.'

I pressed the button. Lots of lights came on and went off and within five seconds I'd lost.

'Play me, play me.'

'Shutup.'

'Play me, play me.'

'I'm warning you.'

The door flew open and in from the storm came a beard, a corduroy jacket, a pipe, and a copy of the previous day's newspaper. The man wrapped up in all this sat on a bar stool and folded the paper around the crossword.

I said to him: 'I read in yesterday's paper, that you can get cancer from eating or drinking hot foodstuffs too quickly.'

'Really.'

'But then I also read somewhere that you can catch Aids from kissing a fireman.'

'Really.'

'Ever been to the Greek Islands?'

'No,' he said and finished his beer.

I wondered what I'd have done if I'd gone down to my local for a quiet drink and a look at the crossword and a man with a ridiculously coloured pullover had come over and started to talk about Aids and cancer and the Greek islands. I promised myself that if it ever did happen I'd buy him a drink, take him home for dinner, let him stay, and put him in the same room as the au pair.

I ended up in a telephone box, Nurse Grimes on the other end of the line.

'Hello, it's me.'

'You left my grill on.'

'I'm in Berwick upon Tweed.'

'Why aren't you in Lapland?'

'It's a long way, you know.'

'You're not eating your roughage, I can tell.'

'It's not that. I'm having trouble finding Newcastle.'

'Get yourself some vitamin E. It's good for concentration. If that doesn't work buy a leisure map.'

'I miss you.'

'You miss my apple crumble and home made bread and tumble dryer, you mean.'

'Hang on, there are the pips.' I struggled with another coin. The coin slot jammed. The line went dead.

Maybe it was time I bought a map.

The next day was even wilder. I had another fried breakfast – my thirty-fifth fried egg of the journey – while my landlady stood staring out of the window. She coughed from the bottom of her stomach and lit another cigarette: 'You should always go on holiday in England during September,' she said, 'it is the nicest month. Of course the summers were always a lot nicer when I was a girl. I lived in Le Havre. It's the Russians, you know. This weather is all their fault.' The Russians had a lot to answer for this summer.

Two Swedes came down to breakfast. They'd arrived late the night before, on their way to Edinburgh. They switched on the television. Frank Bough filled the screen – and to think

people commented on my pullover. The news was all to do
with the washed out Bank Holiday. In the Notting Hill
Carnival policemen tried to laugh as young blacks ran round
with their helmets on and ten thousand revellers tried to
shelter under one umbrella. In Wales they'd had their worst
floods for forty years, a hotel was washed away. In the
Yorkshire Dales they'd had the wettest August on record.
There was film of holidaymakers stuck on caravan roofs and
of one man rescued from the top of a telephone kiosk. He said
afterwards: 'I was going to phone for help but the coin box
was jammed.'

The Swedes flicked from channel to channel. Breakfast
television was a revelation to them. Chris de Burgh came on
singing, 'Lady in Reeeeeeeed'. They both got excited: 'He's
very popular in Sweden,' they said.

'Have you ever been to Lapland?' I asked one of them.

'No. No-one in Sweden likes the Lapps. No-one cares
about them.'

'But surely they'll have to take care of them now.'

'Why?'

'Because of the contamination.'

'What contamination?'

'The radioactive cloud from Chernobyl. The one that
rained over northern Scandinavia.'

They looked at me, nonplussed.

'We come from Stockholm. Nobody cares about the
Lapps down there. The Lapps are drunks and troublemakers.
They are unfriendly. They are like gypsies. The Swedish
disown them. No-one in their right mind would want to go
there.'

'I'm on my way there now.'

Silence.

'Why?'

'Charity. Chernobyl disaster fund.'

'My advice is to buy a reindeer hatstand and come straight back.'

The weatherman forecast the hurricane would blow stronger and warned high sided vehicles to keep off the roads. Cycling was a non starter again. I took down the *Man from Uncle Book Number 7, The Radioactive Camel Affair*, and settled down in front of the gas fire.

'Chapter One: Napoleon Solo shielded his eyes against the blazing sun. Under the folds of his burnous, the heavy Mauser automatic ... ' Hang on, hang on. Burnous? What's a burnous. Napoleon Solo was wearing an article of clothing I didn't know the meaning of. ' ... Solo scanned the plateau with aching eyes. Below and behind, the dead land dropped away in parallel ridges of ochre and gamboge ... ' Gamboge!? What the hell was gamboge! I was reading a *Man From Uncle* book and my vocabulary wasn't up to it! I wouldn't have minded but I'd read this one and numbers 1 to 6 when I was at school! I was even a member of the Uncle Club. I used to have a badge and a wallet and a password.

I switched the TV back on. A chef was giving a demonstration of microwave cooking: 'see, it cooks and it browns and you can even get crackling. And stories about it giving you Aids just aren't true.' I flicked through the channels. The Test Match was on, but not the Test Match they were supposed to be playing that day, the covers were never taken off the pitch in that game. The Test Match they were showing was a recording of The West Indies versus England in the summer of '68. It was warm and sunny and Gary Sobers was at the crease. It was true, the summers were better in those days.

The landlady came in, lit a cigarette and said: 'I never could understand cricket.'

'It's easy,' I said. 'Two teams. They take it in turns to bat and to bowl. The team that scores the most runs wins.'

'Non, I still can't understand.'

She was a shy woman who wouldn't stop talking. She always looked as though she was on the verge of saying something controversial, of speaking her mind. She'd purse her lips, look over her shoulder furtively, open her eyes wide and then say something like: 'I never trust a man who lets his shirt-tail flap outside his trousers.'

We did some more staring out of the window at the wet lorries. The only warming sight was the red glow from the ovens of Tom's Fresh Bake bakery over the road – of course, now I remember, when I bent down to pick the rubbish bag up, it wasn't the oven I switched off, it was the boiler. I remember flicking the button so it showed red. I washed up my baked potato plate, packed my stuff into the panniers, checked the doors and windows one last time and then left. The oven was still on. Had been for seven weeks.

It was almost September. Had the summer really come and gone? In Lapland the sun would be sinking noticeably lower each day now. Soon frosts would begin. I'd climb off the boat at Bergen and be greeted by the first snowfall of the season. My morale hit an all time low. There was only one thing for it.

'I'm going into town to get a haircut.' I said.

The hairdresser had a beautiful Geordie accent. I could have listened to her all day. I only went in for a trim, something to inspire me the way the first cut had done all those weeks ago in His and Hers Trendicuts. But each time she said: 'is that enough?' I answered: 'Little bit more.'

'Just passing through are you?' she said.
'Yes.'
'Where you going?'
'Newcastle ... Then over to Norway.'
'Whereabouts in Norway?'
'Bergen.'

'Then where? Is that enough?'

'Bit more. North.'

'Kristiansund?'

'What?'

'It's up the coast, past Alesund.'

'Right, that's where I'm going.'

'Over the Arctic Circle?'

'Yes.'

'Into Lapland?'

'Yes.'

'I've been there. Is that enough?'

'Bit more. What's it like, Lapland?'

'Lovely.'

'You're sure about that, are you?'

'Yes. I went about this time of year. We visited the fishing stations on the islands of Lofoten, the Finnmark plains and a little Orthodox chapel on the Russian frontier. I came back with a reindeer hat stand. They sold loads of them in this little souvenir shop on the North Cape. They have 240 volt sockets with two prongs, so take an adaptor if you want to use your hairdryer. Is that enough?'

'Yes. Fine.'

On the way home I bought two maps. One of Northumberland and one of Norway. When I got back I unfolded Norway on my bed.

It was still possible. I had to be superbly fit by now. From Bergen it was a mere hop, skip and a jump to Trondheim. Then the road was practically straight all the way up to Bodo. A quick burst over the Arctic Circle to Tromso, and then Hammerfest would be on the road signs. I folded the map away and realised it was decision time. Should I continue my quest for the far north, or should I put my bike on the next Intercity 125 and go home and switch my oven off? It was a dilemma I solved only when I looked at myself in the mirror. My hair had been cut like a convict's. Once again my haircut was saying: 'Go to Lapland.'

'Monsier Wallington, come quickly.' It was my landlady. She was standing at the top of the stairs, looking grave.

'What is it?'

'There's something wrong with your bike.'

Downstairs in the living room my bicycle was still propped up against the wall, but there was something peculiar about it. It slouched, listed, looked ill. Looking down I noticed a flat tyre. My landlady was full of remorse, but I didn't find it a grievous sight. The air slipping slowly out wasn't so much a leak as a long sigh of relief.

She was still concerned the next morning. She stood over me passing me bowls of water and tools as I repaired the puncture and prepared to leave.

'It doesn't seem possible,' she said. 'You're the first guest I've ever had stay who's had a puncture in my living room. I don't know what to say.'

'It's all right, don't blame yourself. It's not your fault. Could have happened to anyone.' Although I had to admit I was baffled. During the last month I'd taken that bike over mountains and moors, along beaches and cinder tracks, through rivers and breakers' yards and yet the first puncture it has is in a living room with nothing for company but a rubberplant and 24 inch black and white Ferranti television. I'd write to *Cycling News* about this one.

Then I was out on the street, the door to the warm haven where I'd weathered out the Bank Holiday firmly closed behind me.

But I felt more confident that morning. My first puncture was out of the way; I felt baptised. I also had a leisure map. And I had renewed conviction. I planned to catch the boat from Newcastle the following evening, and with my revised schedule I calculated I'd arrive at the North Cape in three weeks time, on September 15th at 4.30 p.m. precisely, although with the wind behind me now, as I headed south along the A1, I reckoned I might even make it by 4.00.

8. Northumbria: That Annoying Squeak

And then suddenly I had a job.

I was sheltering in a library, sodden and smelling of diesel when a man with a military moustache came up to me and said:

'Psst.'

'What?'

'Want a job?'

I was in the North East, the unemployment blackspot of the country and yet here was a pukka old boy offering me work.

'What kind of job?'

'Picking fruit.'

'Yes, all right.'

It had taken only a few brushes with juggernauts that morning to realise I couldn't possibly start cycling again until the storm had properly blown itself out, and I figured I might as well pick fruit as hang around libraries. He only wanted me for the day anyway, and so I threw my bike in the back of his van and we drove off to his plantation. 'Are you in the army?' he said.

'No.'

'Just wondered.'

I was part of a team of ten pickers. Nine women and myself. They'd been together all summer, from the strawberry crop through the gooseberries and the plums and now onto the raspberries, and yet they still called each other by their surnames.

The farmer, known to all as the Captain, introduced me. 'This is Mrs Drummond, this is Mrs Casey and that's all I can remember. This is ... this is ... what did you say your name was?'

'Mark.'

'Are you in the army?' said Mrs Drummond.

'No.'

'Just wondered.'

The fruit couldn't be picked when it was raining, so the morning shift was spent sheltering in the caravan. Then we took our lunchbreak sheltering in the caravan, followed by the afternoon shift which was spent sheltering in the caravan. It sounded like a cushy job until I discovered it was piecework.

But when the rain did stop and the work could begin, these demure Northumbrian housewives dived into the raspberry canes like women possessed. The Capt. gave me a tray of punnets to fill. 'And don't go putting any stones in the bottom,' he said.

That was obviously the first trick new workers learnt. But at £1 paid for every 8lbs of raspberries picked you had to have some kind of fiddle. Mine was to put as many raspberries in my mouth as I put in the box.

I was slow at the job and found it back-breaking. For the women though, it was routine and as mindless as conveyor belt work.

'Arthur's getting curious about Pauline isn't he?' said Mrs Howarth.

'It's these creative expression classes she's going to. It's obvious what she's up to,' said Mrs Drummond.

'She won't leave him.'

'She will.'

'She won't.'

'She will.'

'Well, if she does Pete and Kathy are in for a shock when they come home from Holiday.'

Having watched TV for the last two days in Berwick, I realised they were talking about Eastenders.

'I prefer Crossroads,' said Mrs Lamb. 'It's more believable.'

'Coronation Street is the best though,' said Mrs Ayres. 'It's shown in Australia.'

'I prefer the Dallas and Dynasty type,' said Mrs Moffat. 'For the dresses of course.'

The Capt. was feeling left out. 'What's happening in the Archers?' he said.

All the women laughed. Someone said she didn't think it was on any more.

'Elizabeth has passed one of her A-levels and is thinking of opening a boutique,' I told him.

The rain began again and the day's work ended. But the Capt. was well pleased, almost all his crop had been gathered. He called us into the caravan to hand out wages.

The man's mathematics were appalling. The women sat giggling as he tried to work out fractions of raspberries. I earned £3.48 for the day.

The rain continued. The caravan shuddered in the wind. Someone passed round a Thermos flask. Mrs Ayres was reading a magazine with a picture on the front of Boris Becker holding aloft the Wimbledon trophy.

'Boom Boom Becker,' she said.

'I read somewhere you get cancer from drinking your tea too quickly,' said Mrs Nelligan.

'I heard you can catch Aids from a secondhand hot water bottle,' said Mrs Casey.

I suggested we had an End of The Picking Season party, but the idea was met with an awkward silence. Only the Capt. smiled at me and leaning back in his chair he recounted how they used to have parties at the end of the picking season years ago.

'I remember one in particular,' he said, 'one hot night, the last in August. We'd had a bumper crop that year. My wife had made a punch, and some sausage rolls and sandwiches, and all sorts of titbits, and all my pickers dressed up and came to the party on the lawn in front of the big house.'

One or two of the pickers were starting to shuffle their feet and look uncomfortable.

'I'd not seen anyone without their working clothes on before. I couldn't recognise them without a basket of fruit in their hands.' Then his eyes grew shiny and he smiled the wistful smile of someone who's just remembered something particularly special. 'I remember Mrs Bruton looked especially attractive that night.'

The women were all looking at the floor. Here was an occasion no-one wanted to talk about.

'We ended up dancing on the gravel drive. Of course we'd had an awful lot of punch by then.'

Mrs Howarth blushed. It was obvious why there were no more picking parties.

The Capt. wiped the window and looked out at his bare plantation. 'Is it my imagination,' he said, 'or were the summers warmer and sunnier in those days?'

Leisure maps are amazing things, stuffed with information, and essential if you wish to know how far you are from a dry ski-slope, or dolphinarium. Since Berwick I'd planned my route round such attractions, and managed to plot a course that successfully avoided them all. Name any stately home, wildlife sanctuary, or restored watermill in Northumbria and I've not been there.

However, the castle and priory ruins I was heading towards now were rather special. They were on Holy Island, or Lindisfarne, the grey silhouette in the distance, connected to the mainland at low tide by a causeway. I tried cycling over it but the wind coming at me broadside just bowled me over. So I walked, head down, noticing that there were no squashed hedgehogs on this road, only squashed jelly fish.

Holy Island is a natural place of pilgrimage, the site where Christianity first settled in England on a lasting basis. Throughout the dark ages the kingdoms in the north and south of the country were partially converted to Christianity but readily lapsed when confronted by the combined pagan armies. Northumbria however decided to make a stand. Under their king Oswald, and thanks to the work of a Scottish monk named Aidan, a monastary was founded on Lindisfarne in the seventh century. It was destroyed by the Danes in the ninth century but a priory was later built and ruins of that still remain. The most prominent building on the island though is the Lindisfarne Castle. Built in about 1550, it was redesigned into a private residence by Sir Edwin Lutyens ...

'Says here we're not going to get another good summer for 200 years,' said a man reading the *Star*. – I was doing what I normally did when I visited places of historic interest: sitting in a cafe reading a guide book.

'Don't want to believe what you read in the papers,' said his wife, and then they covered themselves in blue water-proofs and struggled outside. I thought about following them. I could see castle-like outlines through the veil of mist and rain and they looked impressive. But I was probably best staying put. If I went any closer I might lose the spiritual glow I presently felt for Holy Island sitting in this cafe.

All day long I followed the coast. It felt strange to be heading south, but I wasn't going to let Newcastle out of my sights now. It was there in large letters at the bottom of the map and I stared at it as I cycled along. In this manner I managed to miss the memorial to Grace Darling, the heroine of the RNLI and a local woman. And I very nearly did the same thing with Bamburgh Castle, a stark collection of crimson walls and turrets, as conspicuous as a power station, standing on its hill staring majestically out to sea, I only stopped there because I collided headlong with the thing, the result of my staring at my map trying to work out what the little red figures signified, the ones that looked like a chef holding up a plate, running across the Landscape. They turned out to be Little Chef restaurants.

The consequences of a collision with walls 11 feet thick would, one could assume, have a profound effect on a bicycle. But my machine was by now fit and well oiled. It could brush Twelfth Century castle keeps aside with ease. The only after effect I noticed was an annoying squeak coming from the front axle. So I unscrewed the wheel, oiled it, screwed it back on again, threw away the washers left over and continued. So did the squeak, but this time on my back wheel.

That evening I reached Seahouses, a scruffy little resort, full of smoking chimneys and advertisements for chimney sweeps. A few tourists huddled together on the front, staring out to the horizon where the battle for The Farne islands raged. You could just make the rocks out, and the lighthouse standing up to the full fury of the North Sea.

But seahouses had a cosy high-walled harbour, which provided shelter from the storm for a fleet of fishing boats and for me to take the back wheel off my bike. I examined the hub, oiled it, relocated it, and the squeak moved on. Moved on to my crank that is.

At five thirty the streets were suddenly full as all the visitors hurried from the shelter of their holiday homes into the fish and chip restaurants that lined the main street. I wiped my oily hands on my trousers and went into one place attracted by the menu-speak on the window: 'A gently fried piece of haddock hidden in a bed of lettuce, fortressed by a garnish of cress, with a compliment of tomatoes.' When the meal arrived I didn't know whether to eat it or frame it.

Then, the next morning the storm had passed. The sky was a battered blue and I cycled gently out of Seahouses past a man carrying black dustbin bags down to the bottom of his drive.

'Keeps you fit,' he said.

'What does?'

I'd stopped, wanting to savour this first conversation of the day, but my response rather threw the gentleman with the plastic bags. He'd said 'keeps you fit' as a throw away. He wasn't expecting to have to elucidate.

'Er ... cycling, I mean,' he said. 'It keeps you fit.'

'Yes.'

'Pedalling and all that. It keeps you fit. Not taking out the dustbins. I didn't mean that keeps you fit. It doesn't. Well, not very fit. Not unless you did it all day long, and then you'd be a dustman, wouldn't you, and they never look fit. No, cycling keeps you properly fit. Cycling does.'

'Yes.'

We were having difficulty establishing common ground. He was emptying dustbins. I was cycling. I couldn't think of anything to say that would combine the two, except perhaps: 'If this squeak doesn't go soon I'm going to throw my bike away.' Now he was standing there, wondering why I'd stopped and what he was going to say next. I didn't want to move on until I'd extracted something from him, some eccentricity of the Northumberland coast, or something about his childhood, how his father worked down the shipyards for twenty years and had fish paste in his sandwiches every day, or, how winning the football pools wouldn't change his life one iota.

He said: 'I mean, cycling doesn't give you cancer or anything.'

'No.'

'Or Aids.'

'No.'

He breathed in the fresh sea air. 'I read in the paper the other day that you can catch Aids from eating improperly defrosted chicken.'

And there it was, the little gem that made the whole interlude worthwhile.

I continued down the coast through the aftermath of the hurricane. Trees lay across the road, the ditches were full of green leaves. And at Beadnell, the bay looked as though a battle had been fought there. Many boats had been sunk or capsized and the beaches were a mess of seaweed and assorted wreckage. One casualty of the storm was a sea bird the size of a dog sitting motionless on the sands, crouched and trying to hide within itself. As I approached all it could do was swivel its head and open its mouth in a plaintive snap. The animal was grounded. Four days of struggling against the gales had exhausted it and now it just sat there looking desperately vulnerable.

The road cut inland here but the tide was out and so I pushed my bike along the firm sand, the squeak now coming from the area around the saddle. 'Annoying squeaks can be eradicated with oil, normally,' said my maintenance book, 'although some are best just ignored and they will go away.' I decided to ignore mine.

'What's that squeaking?' said a man, leaning on his gate.

'What squeaking?'

'That squeaking coming from your bike?'

'I can't hear any squeaking.'

'It's coming from your saddle.'

'No you're mistaken.'

'It's coming from your back axle now.'

'No, you're hearing things.'

'Where are you heading, any road?'

'Newcastle.'

'Newcastle, eh! Well in that case you'd better come and have a look at my hens'.

He led me down a path to his garage. 'I used to live in Manchester, see. Hens are very popular there.' He opened the garage door. The air smelt of the salt breeze and chicken dung. 'A friend of mine in Didsbury kept seventy. Mayor's wife had a couple as well.'

He switched the light on, and there strutting proudly about their coops were his prize birds, brilliantly coloured in the electric light, one pure white, another feathered like a parrot. He picked up a cock, and stroked it lovingly, the bird had just won him second prize in a show. 'I can't understand anyone not wanting to keep hens,' he said, his eyes watery, then the thing crapped all down his jacket.

'See the white one. That's Walter. I'm giving him to my niece. She lives in Newcastle. I'd be ever so grateful.'

'I'm on a bike.'

'Walter wouldn't object. You could put him in a box and strap it to your luggage rack and put a sticker on the back: "Caution Show Hens in Transit." and another on the front: "Beware. I Stop for Hens." He'd be ever so good company. You're never alone with a hen, you know.'

'No, I don't think so.'

'I'd give you some feed and tell you his particularities ...'

'No, I really don't think ... '

' ... how he doesn't like supermarket millet or Mantovani. ... '

'Ah, but I love Mantovani, you see. We'd have nothing in common.'

'Oh, fair enough, then. I'll post him Red Star.'

I climbed back on my bike.

He said: 'that squeak's coming from your front sprocket now, you know.'

'What squeak?'

Another castle was in view, Dunstanburgh according to my leisure map, no doubt as imposing and as strategically important as Bamburgh in days gone by, but now in ruins. And yet castles always look more emotive in ruins. I always feel sorry for them if they've just had their walls repointed, or had plastic guttering put up or if there's a BP tanker outside filling up the central heating reserve. Dunstanburgh looked splendid standing gaunt on a cliff, dark and broken, the wind whistling round its enormous walls. The only influence of the twentieth century was a Cadbury's Flake wrapper lying in the gatehouse.

I'd always wanted to visit this Northumbrian coast and I found it refreshingly untampered with. There was the occasional aberration like Seahouses, but otherwise it was just empty beaches and fishing villages, some like Low Newton, so neat you felt you had to wipe your feet before you walked down to the harbour, and others like Craster still full of boats and dunnage and fishermen, and the smell of kippers from the local smoking sheds.

And the traffic was light. I could tell from the noticeable shortage of squashed animals on the road, also by the complete unawareness of the highway code displayed by the resident wildlife. Just outside Howick I came across a toad, ambling contentedly across the road. I stopped and let it cross in front of me, but there was a car approaching and if the toad didn't hurry it was going to have its dimensions severely altered. I went to pick it up but it leapt further into the danger area. And now the car was just fifty yards away and the toad was beginning to panic, croaking in toad-like fashion and hopping round in circles as if one foot was nailed to the tarmac. I decided to take control and with an outstretched hand brought the approaching vehicle to a halt. The driver wound down his window.

'What's going on?' he said in a voice befitting someone who has just bought himself a D reg. Ford Sierra.

I said: 'Sorry about the delay, sir. There's a toad crossing.'

He got out and we stood over the toad as it slowly hopped over to the verge, encouraged by cries of the:'c'mon you little bastard. I'm supposed to be in Alnwick by 2.30!' variety.

I stayed in Alnmouth that night, partly because it seemed like one of the prettiest towns I'd come across the whole summer, and also because just before I got there the skies turned suddenly black and I was soaked in the daily downpour. I'd planned on sleeping out that night but there I was as usual sitting in a cosy guest house reading the local paper, the rain playing a familiar tune on the roof.

'Recent storms have driven a record number of rare birds onto the eastern seaboard of Great Britain,' said the front page news. 'Wrynecks, Small Brown, Buff and Grey Woodpeckers, have been amongst those forced down while emigrating from Scandinavia to Africa.' I knew how they felt. My journey was in the opposite direction but the weather had played a similarly decisive role in its progress. I thought of that big bird stranded on the beach at Beadnell and I felt just as helpless.

In between cloudbursts I went for a walk along the beach. I thought I might spot one of these rare birds, although I wouldn't have recognised a Wryneck or Buff coloured Woodpecker if one had bit me. I could, however, identify the two dogs running together at speed up and down the beach. They could only be greyhounds.

'Those greyhounds can't half run,' I said to the man exercising them.

'They're whippets,' he said.

'Reckon it's going to rain again?'

'No. Are you in the army?'

'No.'

'Just wondered.'

We stood there surveying the blackening sky. The beach was black as well, tons of seaweed had smothered it.

'That seaweed stinks,' I said.

'It may stink but it's right good for the garden.'

'Seen any rare seabirds?' I asked.

'No. Are you an ornithologist?'

'No.'

''Cos if you were I was going to say you'd have enjoyed that programme last night on the telly. About Peter Scott it was. He used to shoot birds before he started conserving them, you know.'

His whippets were racing up and down the sand by the water's edge. They seemed to grow longer as they ran.

'Are you an ornithologist?' I said.

'Me? No. Mind you, one of the best days of my life was when a pelican almost nested in the shed that's nearly in my back garden.'

We stood in silence and watched the dogs get smaller in the distance. He called them back. 'They're too old to race now,' he said.

The weather moved in again. He said: 'The clouds get whipped across the neck of the country from the Irish sea. This is the narrowest part of England, you see. It's a corridor of climatic change. I read that somewhere. Oh, oh. It's starting again. I'm going inside. The rain makes my hair go all curly.' He hurried off into a caravan up on the low cliff. His dogs followed. I was left there to get drenched again. 'Bye,' I said. 'See you again,' and I thought: I must stop saying 'see you again' to people I'm never going to see again.

Thanks to my leisure map, I'd become a *bona fide* tourist overnight. I never so much as went to the lavatory now without first consulting my map for the nearest public convenience. And I suddenly discovered I was mixing with tourists as well. Not that that made the trip any less interesting. One member of the family on holiday I met in Alnmouth that night was one of the most extraordinary characters I'd met all summer.

His name was Michael and he was three years old. His father introduced us. There was something strange about the way his father spoke; it wasn't until he said he came from Guildford that I realised it was his Southern accent; I hadn't heard one for so long and now it seemed so expressionless and unexciting. But then what the man was talking about didn't exactly inspire expression and excitement. Like most people who live on the periphery of London, his small talk revolved around the M25.

'You see, traffic flow over the next twenty-five years was supposed to have been evaluated and the motorway constructed accordingly, but you've only got to drive from Guildford to Leatherhead to realise ... '

'Daddy ... '

'Yes. What?' Michael was tugging at his father. He wore shoes with Left and Right written on them.

'Are we still on holiday?'

'Yes Michael we're still on holiday ... and what's absolutely ridiculous is that there's no motorway service on the whole 121 miles. Lighting isn't up to much either. There's 25% more chance of an accident ... '

'Daddy! ... ' Michael had moved to the other side of the room and was shouting.

'Yes ... what?'

'If I stand over here am I still on holiday?'

Michael's problem was that he hadn't fully grasped the concept of holidays. He couldn't identify them as abstract entities. If one minute he was on holiday and then the next he wasn't there had to be a crossover point he deduced.

'Yes son, you're still on holiday ... now if only they could abolish toll booths at Dartford Tunnel, Well, what a difference that would make.'

'Are we still on holiday when we go to our room?'

'Yes.'

'But we weren't on holiday when we were in the kitchen in Guildford this morning?'

'No.'

So what was the difference between being in the kitchen in Guildford and being in room number six of the Farne View Guest House, Alnmouth? No, he couldn't puzzle it out.

It had been the coldest August night for twenty years my radio announced as I passed the Caribbean restaurant in Shilbottle where you could get Hot White Man for £5.50 and Steak Gumbo for £6.70. I clearly wasn't going to make the Friday night boat from Newcastle now, I'd have to catch the Monday one, so I had the weekend. I also still had that squeak. It had settled on my front brakes now. The maintenance book said: 'Squeaking brakes are annoying and can be cured by cleaning the wheel rim with benzine or by toeing the brake shoes.' I did this and the squeak moved to the back brakes. 'If squeak persists, ignore it and it will probably go away.' After a mile the squeak did go away as predicted. After two miles it returned, now housed somewhere in my steering column.

The coldest August night in twenty years deserved a twenty year old song the DJ decided and so I cycled on to the Edwin Hawkins singers and 'Oh Happy Days' until I reached the village of Long Framlington. I would have passed straight through, but like a Hamelin rat I was drawn towards the sound of pipe music, not because it was irresistible but because it was the least tuneful noise I'd ever heard and I wanted to meet the person responsible.

My ears led me to a Northumbrian Pipe manufacturer's workshop. Inside, a man stood in the corner of the room with a spider-like contraption tucked under his arm. Pipes stuck out of it from all angles and from somewhere near his armpit came a baleful noise reminiscent of small furry animals being strangled. He came to the end of the piece and said: 'That was called, "Swindon, oh Swindon".'

I thought it summed up Swindon rather nicely but his tutor was far from happy with the rendition.

'You're not playing the music, only the notes!' he said. 'To play the Northumbrian pipes you have to feel them.' Then he slapped his forehead and returned to his workshop and started hammering things.

'He's a bit temperamental,' said the piper. 'All geniuses are. He never even listened to "Norwich I Miss You So". And I've been practising that all week.'

Before he got ideas about playing it to me I asked him what the map on the wall was for. It was of the world and had black and red pins stuck all over it.

He said: 'The red pins are the places where he's sold Northumbrian pipes.'

'And the black pins?'

'Er ... the black pins are where he ran out of red pins.'

The pipes had been sold all over the globe, and there at the top of the board was a pin stuck in the middle of Lapland.

'Very popular in Scandinavia, Northumbrian Pipes are,' he said, and did more to dampen my enthusiasm for the place than any amount of radioactivity.

I asked him if many people still played the pipes and he said that in this village alone there were once twenty players, but they all got married and moved South: 'They'll be lots playing tomorrow at the Bellingham Show though. They're having a Northumbrian Pipes contest.'

I'd heard much talk about the forthcoming Bellingham Show. It was the local event of the year. A date in everyone's calendar, when the best of everything from Blackface Sheep to dropped scones went on display.

'You should come along,' he said. 'Everyone will be going. Everyone that is except Jack Carey.'

'Why won't Jack Carey be going?'
'Someone got into his garden and stole his leeks.'
'What did Jack say to that?'
'He said the thief's as good as dead.'
'He treats thieves violently does he?'
'No, but he treats his leeks with fungicide.'

He was right. Everyone was in Bellingham for the show. The pubs were a strange mixture of farmers dressed for the sheep and cattle contests, and teenagers dressed up for the Eve of Show disco. Four girls from the latter group sat down next to me in the Black Bull as I had some supper. One of them squashed right up to me and blew Embassy Regal smoke all over my quiche and chips.

'Sorry,' she said, and blew the next lungful into my salad.

I offered them a chip each. They took one and the girl in the purple and green off the shoulder number said:

'Are you in the army?'

'No.'

'Just wondered. We're a bit overexcited. We're going to the dance. Is that your best pullover?'

A team of men had walked in. I asked the girls what the local men were like.

'Bunch of wankers,' said the sweet young thing in a lemon coloured leotard.

The girls giggled and waved coyly. The men ignored them and moved as one to the bar where they ordered pints of lager, 'in straight glasses'. They all had sharp bums and noses and thin moustaches, and they stood in a circle with one hand round a pint and the other in a pocket.

One of the girls took off her cardigan to reveal an expanse of back. 'It's like an oven in here,' she said, and I immediately thought about my oven at home – maybe I switched it off when I came back up the stairs to ... – but then I realised I didn't care any more.

I walked with them to the dance, and I would have gone in but as the door opened I heard Chris de Burgh and I think I'd rather have danced to Swindon, Oh Swindon.

'I love this song,' all the girls said.

I wished them goodnight and as I walked off one of them called out: 'Your shoes are right squeakers aren't they.'

The next day I went to the show with Ted from the lodgings I'd found. I told him I was a telephone engineer.

'I'm a telephone engineer as well,' he said.

'Yeah, well let's not talk shop.'

'Just passing through, eh? You'll like Bellingham. If you stay here the weekend I guarantee you'll get off with one of the local girls.'

We walked down to the show ground. It was muddy and cold. The chill wind made my nose run. We bought a programme and a raffle ticket each for a 12″ black-and-white Television and headed off for the sheep ring.

'Yes, you'll like Bellingham, all right,' said Ted. 'Doesn't concern me now, of course, I'm married, but when I first came to live here I couldn't believe it. The scandal in this village is nobody's business. You think London is wild? You should spend some time here. There's one chap in the village who reckons he's got Aids. Tell you what, let's go and say hello to Derek Gibbs. By the way do you know you squeak?'

It was true. One of the girls had noticed it last night. And now I could hear it. I squeaked as I walked. I'd caught it off my bike. It had started in my feet then worked its way up to my knee but had now moved to my shoulder. Ignore it and it'll go away; that's what the maintenance book had said.

In the sheep pens a selection of immaculately manicured animals were coralled, their fleeces combed, horns filed, tails scrubbed. The farmers stood proudly by them, burly countrymen dressed in their Sunday best jacket and cap, and clutching a crook.

Derek Gibbs was the one who looked like Max Bygraves. 'Hello Ted,' said Derek, 'coming to the beer tent?'

He led us through the crowds to the beer tent: 'Two double scotches for my friends,' he called to the barman. 'Here, got a joke for you. What's brown and sounds like a bell? Give up? Dung! Ha. Shepherd's joke, that.'

Ted went to the Gents and Derek Gibbs began to tell me how his wife would never listen to his jokes, how things weren't going well in their marriage and how sheep were an escape for him. I repeated this to Ted a while later when we were watching the Cumberland and Westmorland wrestling bouts. Ted seemed amazed.

'Funny really, people telling you, a complete stranger, their marital problems.'

'Yes.'

One fat man and one thin man walked out into the ring. It looked an unfair confrontation. And yet the thin man was supple and quick. He danced around the fat man. He looked wily. The fat man couldn't turn as gingerly. The thin man bounced off the ropes, slapped the fat man on the cheeks, teased him, and tired him, always staying just out of his grasp. Then, picking his moment he grabbed the fat man and went to swing him over his shoulder. But the fat man picked him up, threw him to the floor and sat on him. Contest over.

'Yep, I find that really funny,' said Ted.

'What?'

'People telling you, a complete stranger, about their marriages breaking up. Funny really. I'd find it difficult to talk to a stranger about my marriage, which isn't going that well as it happens.'

We threaded our way through the goats, the chickens and the cattle, all looking ridiculously well-groomed. A cow just didn't look right with a pristine backside. Many animals were already decorated with rosettes, the horses in particular. There were competitions for shetlands, for heavy horses, for dray horses, horses in fancy dress, hunters and jumpers. The most popular attraction though was the mechanical Rodeo Poneo. It seemed most spectators prefered to see riders thrown than have clear rounds.

In the horticultural and home crafts tent, the local home bakers had prepared a feast of shortbread, scones, cakes and gingerbread men. It was a mouthwatering display and I just wanted to try it all. But the only way you could taste any was to be a judge. They walked round taking supercilious nibbles, and then wrote such comments as, 'could have done with an extra half hour.' It was all desperately frustrating. The only food for sale was hamburgers.

And next to the baking were the vegetable and flower displays. More of a freak show than anything else. There'd be the biggest leek you'd ever seen lying on a table and there next to it there'd be a bigger one. An onion the size of a football sat on a handkerchief, not a speck of dirt on it, even its roots were combed out, and yet it had only won third prize. And prizes were what these shows were all about. There was a fierce sense of competition prevailing. This was the chance to show off that everyone had waited the whole season for, and they wanted it to be official. The rosette for the best marrow or the best dahlia was something you could proudly put on your mantlepiece for the next year.

Alternatively you could pin it to your jacket as Derek Gibbs had done that night.

Determined to prove to me what a den of iniquity Bellingham was, Ted had taken me to the Rose and Crown where Derek stood propping up the bar, his rosette for third prize trailing in his beer. 'Two double scotches for my friends,' he called to the barmen. 'Here, got another joke for you.' But he was drunk and kept forgetting the story. I thought he'd finished three times and laughed politely. 'I like you,' he said. 'You understand my jokes. My wife doesn't. But then she doesn't understand sheep either.'

Ted dragged me off. He wanted to take me to the Fox and Hounds. 'And you say people are always telling you their marriage problems?'

'Not always, now and again it's happened on this trip.'

'Amazing that is. I could never tell a stranger my marriage problems. Not that I've got any major ones, it's just that well ... you're still squeaking, you know?'

The squeak had now lodged in my neck. Every time I turned my head it sounded like a door opening. I couldn't ignore it much longer.

The Fox and Hounds had all the qualities of a condemned building. The woodwork was coming off the walls, the plaster crumbling, holes were covered with cardboard. It seemed as though someone had gone to great lengths to make it as uncomfortable a place to spend a Saturday night as possible, yet so full of people was it you could hardly move to scratch your nose:

'A good job we came here early. It gets busy after ten,' said Ted, joining the scrum at the bar.

The reason it got busy after ten was that scotch was half price then and the whole village elbowed its way in. And scotch was all that was served. There was some brown coloured water sitting in a jug on the bar but no-one touched it. Beer was available but they pulled it begrudgingly, and they still talk about the time a tourist came in and asked for a Slimline Bitter Lemon and a packet of dry roasted.

We pushed our way into the back room where a piano was being played. Although, played might not be the right verb here. There was a woman sitting at the stool fingering the keys, but not in any sort of sequence, she just hit them in time. Not that it would have made much difference had she been Elton John, the piano had three generations of beer inside it and once struck a key stayed down for the evening.

'That's my auntie, playing that,' said a big, brown woman with no shoes on.

I said: 'it's very ... very ... er ... it's very,' and that was all the encouragement she needed. She grabbed me and dragged me onto the two foot square piece of lino in the middle of the room which acted as a dance floor and already had four couples on it: 'Let's dance,' she said, 'I've just come back from Corfu and I'm pissed.' And she clutched me to her bosom, breathed Barcardi all over me, thrust a leg between mine and swung me round to the tune of 'Two Lovely Black Eyes'.

'Are you in the army?' she said.

'No.'

'Well how come you've got that ridiculous haircut?'

'My Bonnie lies over the ocean,' sang the pianist.

'Don't play that, Auntie. Play "Roll Out The Barrel".'

'Roll out the barrel,' sang her auntie, although she didn't bother to play a different tune.

'Told you you'd be all right in Bellingham,' said Ted with a wink, as the big, brown, drunk woman who'd just come back from Corfu put her other leg between mine and swung me round again.

'How are you making that squeaking noise?' she said.

But she hadn't realised what she'd taken on when she commandeered me on the dance floor. With my unmatching feet and complete lack of rhythm, I've broken the morale and the ankles of ethnic dancers, professional and amateur, all over Europe. There's a Portuguese folk dancer on the Algarve who'll never walk properly again, and that flamenco dancer in Seville was fortunate her legs were heavily insured. And now there was this poor woman from Bellingham who was still dancing on taverna courtyards to the balalaika with wasp-waisted Greek waiters on warm bougainvillea-scented evenings in the Cyclades. 'This is how Spiros used to do it,' she cried, and I got carried away and the next time she swung me round I came down hard on what I thought was the floor but turned out to be her bare feet.

There was a crunch of bone and a crossing of eyes and I was suddenly dancing on my own.

Ted came back with two more double whiskies. 'What did you say to her? She's out there in tears. Did she tell you about her broken marriage?'

'No.'

'No, and I wouldn't either, not that my marriage is on the verge of breaking up or anything. Come here, I want you to meet Ivor.'

Ivor was from Newcastle. He spoke broad Geordie and we had a fascinating conversation which I didn't understand a word of. How he got his throat round the sort of angles he did, I'll never know. Every now and then I'd be able to guess from his intonation he was asking a question and so I'd try to look indecisive and say: 'Maybe.' From what I could gather he wanted me to go down to Blackpool with him the following weekend with a bunch of his mates: 'No sleep, no food, just forty-eight hours booze, what do you say?'

'Maybe.'

After getting little sense out of me for half an hour. He looked at me and said: 'Are you foreign?'

'Maybe.'

'Is that why you're squeaking?'

Ted and I were the last to leave. We collected the empty glasses for the owner. She'd inherited the pub three years ago from her father who had fought all his life to keep the big brewers from turning it into a chicken and chip place like the other pubs in the village. She wanted to keep the tradition going, but she knew unless some money was raised for repairs the place would soon fall down around her.

'It's not entirely my decision, see,' she said. 'This place was left a third to me and a third each to my nephew and ... and ... what's that other thing?'

'Niece.'

'That's it, niece. And my nephew and niece want the brewers to move in.'

It seemed ridiculous that the money couldn't be raised by other means. Across the road in St Cuthbert's church, the roof needed restoration and the appeal fund was gradually climbing up to the five thousand pound target. Whereas the Fox and Hounds, which was just as fundamental a part of the village fabric, was going to be condemned soon for want of half that cost. It wouldn't need anything flashy like a coat of paint or the piano fixing, just a damp course and someone in to fix the dry rot. I said: 'You should have a pub restoration fund and have one of those target displays hung outside. And have coffee mornings and a pub garden fete, jumble sales and bring and buy bazaars, and quiz evenings and raffles for fridge freezers and lawn mowers and ... just a thought.'

'You're drunk,' she said and closed the door on us.

Ted and I stood outside. It was another clear and frosty August night. He said:

'I never spoke to you about my marriage did I?'

'No. I never told you I was going to Lapland did I?'

'No. Actually, I'm not sure if I want my marriage to continue. It's gone far enough.'

'That's exactly how I feel about Lapland.'

'I'll give it one last try.'

'Same here.'

We walked back to the house; the sky was full of stars. 'Look how low in the sky the plough is,' said Ted. 'Sign of winter, that is. Your squeak's gone, by the way.'

9. Newcastle: Touring

I was in the village of Wark, sitting on the coronation bench, the one dedicated to Bruce Douglas. The day was warm and still and there was thunder in the air.

'We should be thankful we don't control the weather,' said one of the Sunday papers, 'think of the conflict between farmer and tourist.' What conflict? If we could control the weather we could have it raining over the farmers' fields and sunny over the picnic sites and beaches, there'd be no conflict there. This trip had taught me life is often a lot more straight forward than it seems. And never had it been more straightforward than it was that morning. Over the last six weeks I'd collected together all the equipment I needed for survival in Lapland. In my panniers now was everything from spare spokes to instructions on how to catch fish through holes in the ice. My bicycle was that-once-dreamed-of 'precision piece of engineering not unlike the human body'. And my body was a precision piece of engineering not unlike the bicycle. This preparatory stage of the journey was now complete. I had new batteries in my radio and Status Quo were on in stereo, and there was nothing but a few miles between me and the boat to Bergen.

A coach from Jolly Bros. trundled past. Travel the Jolly Way, it had emblazoned on the side. And that's just what I did all the way into Newcastle.

Newcastle had yellow and white buses and advertisements for Newcastle Brown looking down from every street corner. Finally reaching the city felt as though it should have been a momentous event, but it was an anti-climax really. Like every other English city, town or village on a Sunday afternoon, Newcastle was closed.

And I mean really closed. Not only were shops shut and locked, their windows were boarded up or had wire mesh nailed over them. The prevailing atmosphere was of a city under siege, an impression substantiated by the officer on duty in the police station where I stopped to find somewhere to stay. He said:

'You want to get out of Newcastle as quick as you can. Head down the coast to Whitley Bay. How are you travelling anyway?'

'On a bike.'

'On a bike! I should watch out for muggers then. And whatever you do, make sure you find a place to stay where you can keep it in your bedroom. They'll swipe anything in this city. My brother had the back wheel nicked off his bike, which doesn't sound so amazing until you realise he was riding the thing at the time.'

I'd been told Whitley Bay was the North East's Blackpool but it was much more attractive than that. It had wide white beaches with fishing boats hauled up on them, and a thin collection of guest houses straddled along the front. It was more reminiscent of Newquay in Cornwall and parts of it had a maritime feel. One part in particular: the B&B I stayed at. The house had seascapes on every wall, model boats on every shelf. There was a biography of Nelson in the bathroom, and each door was marked with a cabin number. I was in number four – ship's mate.

The owner of the house was a fisherman and the sea was his life. His wife was a counter assistant in Boots, and looked fed up with the whole charade.

He welcomed me aboard with ship's hospitality: 'C'mon

in, sit down. Name's Ron. Have a cup of tea.' He handed me
a Capt. Pugwash mug. 'Not in the Navy are you?'

'No.'

'Just wondered.'

Ron had a strange accent which I put down to a
combination of his Geordie background and the fact he'd just
had two teeth extracted. 'Where are you going?' he said.

'Lapland.'

'Why?' said his wife.

'Charity. RNLI.'

'I thought Lapland had been blown up.'

'No, just severely contaminated with radiation.'

'Oh, that's all right then. Ron's been to Lapland, haven't
you Ron?'

'Aye, I've been to Lapland. Good fishing.'

'What was the land like?' I asked.

'Don't remember any land.'

'He didn't even bring me home an ornamental reindeer
hatstand,' said his wife.

Ron was only home for a couple of days before his boat
went to sea again, but he was already bored. 'We've got a
history of work in the North East, it's our heritage,' which
was why the recession had hit hardest up here. The North
East was built on heavy industry and hard work. The ships,
the steel and the coal were all the people knew. But here, as
all over the North, what had once made the region great had
gone, and they were left scratching their heads.

Ron said: 'In the south if you can't find work you can
always fiddle a living. You can't do that up here. You can't
fiddle money out of people who haven't got any.'

And the saddest thing about this Tyne area was the way
the traces of industry had been swept away. It was a
complete resignation. All the old sites along the river had
been landscaped. The docks were spotless, grassed over and
given the flower tub treatment. The smoke had been blown

away, and the throb of industry working through the night silenced, and in place of it all were mosaics and murals of workers digging coal and welding boats together.

'The highest unemployment in the country up here,' said Ron, 'and Newcastle looks really pretty because of it.'

That night the thunder arrived. The rain pelted on the street. Lightning flashed on the horizon. But come the morning the sun rose out of the sea and zapped against my window pane with a thud. I looked out to see the front washed in gold light and the bay streaked with sunshine. Directly across that water lay Bergen.

At the breakfast table Ron's boy sat dressed in school uniform.

'Why so glum?' I said.

'Back to school today,' said his mother, handing me my thirty ninth fried egg of the trip.

'I spent all summer playing football on the beach and British Bulldog up the alley,' he said, which sounded like a pretty good holiday to me, but seeing schoolkids in uniform again was the most emphatic reminder I could imagine that the summer was over.

Then suddenly these reminders were everywhere. On the roads lollipop ladies were out in force again. The flowers were dead in the hanging baskets. September sales were in the shop windows. 'Lady in Red', was sliding down the charts, the next time I heard it would be on a nostalgia show. The season was officially over and yet this was the warmest, sunniest day of my journey. The North Sea was a deep blue and I walked along the front in a t-shirt remembering all the places I'd sheltered in over the past six weeks. There was that first time in the Worcestershire supermarket; then under the bridge in the Teme valley; in the caravan in Bishops' Castle; under the market hall in Much Wenlock; the stables at Ingestre; the cycle shop in Ashbourne; the umbrella in the well-dressing parade at Bradwell; with Nurse Grimes in the oyster bar in Blackpool; the condemned mill in Bradford; the barn at Malham; the fudge shop in Grassington; that tree near Sedbergh and the other tree a hundred yards further on; the tourist office in Appleby in Westmorland; the beach shelter in Silloth; the church coffee morning in Brampton; the Once Brewed information centre by Hadrian's Wall; the phone box in Hexham; the travel agents in Berwick; the library, bakers, barbers, chip shop and pub also in Berwick; the cafe on Holy Island. I must have been the most sheltered person of 1986.

Later, I cycled down to North Shields, to where the Norway Line terminal was. The boat to Bergen, the MS *Venus*, was there on the water, glinting in the sunlight, much freight and forklift activity at her side. There were Scandinavian licence plates on the trucks and the occasional sing-song Scandinavian accent. At last someone to speak Norwegian to! I approached a lorry driver:

'*Hva koster det til Bergen?*' I asked.

(What's the fare to Bergen?)

'*Jeg har en los tann, jeg vil ikke at De skal trekke den,*' he replied.

(I've a loose tooth, but I don't want it extracted.)

Cars were filing on board. I checked my stuff one last time. I couldn't believe I'd actually organised myself. Then the last call came over the tannoy and I wheeled my bike off towards the ships's hold and began to prepare myself for the big push north.

10. Lapland or Bust

Then I got to Bergen, cycled up to Lapland, bought a reindeer hatstand and came back. It was enormous fun and I can recommend the trip to anyone.

11. Bust

Actually, that last chapter was a lie.

I wheeled the bike out of the terminus and looked across the Tyne to South Shields. Beyond that lay Sunderland and Durham. I'd always wanted to go to Durham.

My problem was I was a lousy traveller. I was too easily distracted. It was obvious at the rate I was going I wouldn't get to the land of the midnight sun until Christmas. I couldn't go on. I didn't even have any lights on my bike.

But somehow Lapland didn't really seem important any more. I think I'd realised that two nights previously in the Fox and Hounds in Bellingham when I suddenly had the sensation of being in a foreign country. I was in a crumbling house on a frosty summer's evening, high in a range of hills, where people were performing strange dances and playing strange music, speaking in strange languages and treating me as though I was from another planet. I never thought travelling through England could provide the same sort of mystery that travel to foreign parts so easily manages but on this journey through the North, the weather, the accents, the landscape and the Northcountry folk had combined to create a land as weird and as wonderful as everything I'd ever hoped Lapland would be. I'd not reached the North Cape but I'd reached North Shields.

I watched the boat set sail, then cycled into the city and caught a train south. It had taken me almost seven weeks to reach Newcastle. Four hours later I was back in London.

12. Hertfordshire: Storing a Bicycle

It was the summer a parrot inherited £5000, the summer the Isle of Rockall moved a mile to the south, the summer the Dutch were officially announced the tallest nation in the world.

None of these or any other earthshattering event had had any effect on The Blue Boar, the pub in St Albans from which I'd cycled away seven weeks previously. In exactly the same corner of the bar stood exactly the same teachers. There was even something familiar about their conversation:

'You see, the keyboard of the 8256 has been set up so that when it's running CP/M, 147 single key or multiple keystrokes produce printable characters, and another 49 produce control codes,' said Charlie Drake.

'Right,' said Bamber Gascoigne.

'But what you must remember is there are some special key combinations which cannot be altered because they affect the way the 8256 operates. These ... '

'Hello.'

'Hello Mark ... these problems will become more evident when you want to produce foreign language text,' said Charlie Drake.

'Right,' said Bamber Gascoigne.

'Now then, the full list of characters available under all the foreign language variations is ... '

'I'm back.'

'What?'

'I'm back. Back from my trip to Lapland. Remember.'

I'd been in a dilemma about what to tell people. I could say
I got to Lapland but it was too painful to talk about. I could
say I got there and then have fabricated the whole trip. I did
after all have an in-depth knowledge of the area. ('Yes, I
found the Lapps a strange and magical people. They have
four hundred different words for reindeer, you know. Their
territory is a crescent of wild country; didn't you get my
postcards? The food was nice. Pickled bear feet are very
tasty. The social life was poor. Lapp skis are 16 centimetres
broad, and 2 metres long. Yes, I'd love to go again. I left my
heart in Hammerfest. *'Hvor er naermeste vaskeri? Jeg vil gjerne ha
disse klaerne presset.'* (Where's the nearest laundry? I want
these clothes pressed.'))

Or I could impress upon people how there was nothing
wrong with a journey just because it failed, – failed that is
merely to reach its destination. Far too many expeditions up
mountains and down rivers were successful. Too many
travellers scaled their peaks and found their sources. There
needed to be more failures. The reasons why someone didn't
get there can be just as appealing as the preplanned, step by
step, by-the-book account of how they arrived at their goal.
Besides, reaching a destination is predictable. It's what you
set out to do. Because I hadn't reached Lapland it still held an
enormous thrill for me. My image of the land and its people
hadn't been tainted by my visiting the place. And anyway, I
didn't need to go all the way to the Arctic Circle to discover
a strange and unexplored land, I'd found one here on my own
doorstep ... etc etc. It all sounded a bit like The Wizard of
Oz on a bicycle, and it would mean that my donation to the
charity I couldn't remember the name of would be reduced
from £2.50 to 35p, but it was the excuse that suited me best.

'Lapland?' said Charlie Drake.

'Yes. You remember I went off to Lapland. On a bicycle. The day of the Royal Wedding.'

'What Royal wedding?'

'You remember, you stood there and said: "give my regards to the Arctic Circle".'

'No, not me, you must be thinking of someone else. Have you joined the army or something?'

'No.'

'Just wondered ... now where was I? Each character is known to the word processor by code, usually represented as a decimal number between 0 and 255 ... '

Ralph was in there on a night off work.

'Hello. I'm back,' I said.

'You ate my Sainsbury's cheese and bacon flan.'

'Yes, sorry.'

'And you left my oven on.'

'Sorry.'

'Where have you been anyway? Haven't seen you around for a week or so.'

'Lapland. Remember.'

'Oh yeh. Lapland.'

'I've been gone seven weeks.'

'Must be your round then.'

One of the people who sponsored me joined us.

'You're back then?'

'Yes.'

'So how was it?'

'Well ... '

'You don't look very brown.'

'Well ... '

'Greek Islands were the hottest place in Europe for all of August, it said in the paper. We went there ourselves. Surprised we didn't see you. Couldn't work out how you were going to cycle there though. We went to Milos. They've got a lovely harbour. Wasn't a cloud in the sky the whole fortnight. Strange bunch the Greeks though, second shortest race in Europe, apparently ... '

'You sponsored me, remember?'

'No, I don't remember that. You must be thinking of someone else. Here, want to but a raffle ticket? Donations to the football team restoration fund.'

Linda came over and smiled: 'So, the wanderer returns.'

'Yes.'

'You've been gone seven weeks.'

'Yes.'

'I never thought you'd get back.'

'No.'

'Did you manage to ... '

'Yes I managed to get there in the end. It was hell, sheer hell. Radioactive reindeer all over the place. No roads, just Tundra and a never ending horizon. Had to carry the bike in places. Had to eat a pedal once. Had innumerable terrifying experiences with bears and things, but I got there in the end.'

'I meant did you manage to get my perfume? Diorissima 90ml atomiser.'

'No. No, I forgot.'

'I forgot to water your plants.'

'Right.'

'And I forgot to renew your library books.'

'Right.'

I went home. As I climbed the stairs, it suddenly all came back to me. After I'd answered the telephone to the wrong number who thought I was Timothy Whites, and then taken the dustbin out and strapped my panniers to my bike, in between switching the immersion heater off and closing the windows, just before writing to DVLC at Swansea and just after I took the dessert spoons from the kitchen drawer, I turned the oven off. I could remember clearly now.

I went into the kitchen. Yep. It was off. Then I went into

the living room and discovered I'd left the stereo on all summer.

I wheeled my bike round to the shed. Tomorrow I must oil it, I told myself. In fact, I should clean it up properly, service it regularly, look after it. I should take up cycling seriously. It was stupid to get this fit and then revert immediately to slobbery. I'd use the bike to explore this area. I'd never taken any interest in Hertfordshire but I was probably underestimating the county. I'd lived here three years and didn't know anything about it. I'd make a point of going on regular rides. Yes, that's what I'd do.

I leant the bike against some cardboard boxes, knowing I'd never get on the thing again. Then I went inside to watch a Bilko repeat.